P9-BBV-138

Juicy

CONFESSIONS OF A FORMER BASEBALL WIFE

Jessica Canseco

ReganBooks

An Imprint of HarperCollins*Publishers*

Juicy

HarperCollins books may be purchased for educational, business, or sales promotional use. For information please write: Special Markets Department, HarperCollins Publishers Inc., 10 East 53rd Street, New York, NY 10022.

FIRST EDITION

Designed by Kris Tobiassen

Printed on acid-free paper

Library of Congress Cataloging-in-Publication Data has been applied for.

ISBN 13: 978-0-06-088945-6
ISBN 10: 0-06-088945-4

05 06 07 08 09 RRD 10 9 8 7 6 5 4 3 2 1

To my wonderful daughter, Josie:

I love you, I am proud of you, and I will always be there for you.

You are the most important person to me, little girl!

Contents

Mr. Gorgeous

At the age of nineteen, when I still knew very little about life and even less about myself, I fell hopelessly in love with the most gorgeous man I had ever seen. It took me the better part of a decade to get over that horrible addiction.

I was a college student at the time, strapped for cash, and Cathleen, one of my housemates, told me about Hooters, the national restaurant chain. She worked at the Cleveland branch, and she said the waitresses made very good money. "You're real pretty, and you have real nice breasts," she observed. "You'll do great."

I went in and filled out an application. The manager glanced at the application, took a considerably long look at my breasts, and asked when I could start. I reported for work that same week, a Hooters trainee. I had to learn the names of about one hundred beers, both the ones on tap and in bottles, and I had to familiarize myself with about a dozen house wines. Those first two days were torture. When someone explains something to me in person, verbally, I'm really quick, and I don't need to hear it twice. But when I'm forced to process written information, it's sheer hell.

I was a terrible waitress. I was so nervous in my tight little Hooters outfit that I kept messing up my orders. I couldn't even keep my tables straight or tell one set of customers from another, but the men never complained. "That's okay, honey. Don't worry about a thing. Why don't you pull up a chair and tell us about yourself?"

On my third day of training, three absolutely gorgeous men walked into the bar. One of them was wearing bright yellow pants and a vibrant red shirt, an outfit that practically screamed for attention. I thought he was the epitome of cool. Then again, that was more than a decade ago, in May 1993, to be specific, back in the days when I was wearing gold-colored shorts and collared Izod shirts, so my own fashion sense left a great deal to be desired. Still, his clothes were the least of it. He was as stunningly handsome a man as I'd ever seen, and he took my breath away.

The man in the yellow pants noticed me, too. "Can I sit at one of your tables?" he asked. He was a perfect gentleman about it, soft-spoken and low-key, but I pointed out that my entire section was full. He suggested I borrow a table from one of the other girls, and that's what I did. "There's this guy and his friends who want to sit in my section," I explained to a fellow waitress. "Would you mind?"

"*This guy*?" she repeated, incredulous. "Don't you know who that is?"

"No," I said.

"It's Jose Canseco," she said.

"Who?"

"*Jose Canseco,*" she repeated. "The baseball player."

It still meant nothing to me. I could have told you more than you wanted to know about Metallica or Pink Floyd, but I didn't know anything about professional sports.

"He's the forty-forty guy," the bartender said, piping up.

"The what?"

He explained that the benchmark of a great season, going back one hundred years, had been thirty home runs and thirty stolen bases, and that Canseco had come along in 1988 and raised the bar with forty home runs and forty stolen bases. At that point in time, no other player had matched his record, and it would still be a few years before Barry Bonds reached the same milestone.

"That's nice," I said, and I went off to show Jose and his friends to an empty table. I smiled my Hooters smile and asked what I could get them.

"How about your phone number?" Jose said, making his eyebrows dance.

"We'll see," I said, trying to be a true professional.

The guys finally ordered—sandwiches, no drinks—and I went to put in their order. When I stopped by the bar to fetch water for the table, the bartender asked me what Jose had said.

"Nothing," I replied. "He asked for my phone number."

"And you blew him off?"

"What was I supposed to do?"

He was incredulous. "It's Jose Canseco!"

One of the waitresses was standing within earshot, shaking her head from side to side. "You don't want to mess with him," she warned me. "He's a wife beater." I didn't know whether that was true, but I knew she was jealous. All the waitresses were ogling Jose and his two friends, including my housemate Cathleen, but I was getting the attention.

When I returned to the table, Jose smiled at me. "So what about that phone number?" he asked.

"Aren't you married?" I asked. I didn't know if he was married, but he couldn't very well be a wife beater without a wife, so I simply assumed he was, whether there was any truth to the ugly rumor.

"No," he said. "I'm divorced."

"Are you sure?"

"Yes."

"Are you really Jose Canseco?"

One of the other players grabbed Jose's hand and showed me a birthmark across the back of it, as if that would somehow confirm his identity. I didn't know who he was, so how was I expected to know he had a birthmark? And it was one butt-ugly birthmark, believe me: a big brown spot about the size of an egg, with fur-like hair growing out of it. It sort of looked like a cockroach. For a moment, I thought about shaving it and drawing little legs along both sides to make it look even more roach-like.

"That's very attractive," I said.

Jose laughed. "Can I take you to lunch sometime?"

"Okay," I said. I didn't think there was any harm in that. I jotted my number on a paper napkin and slid it across the table.

"Thanks," he said, pocketing the napkin. "I'll call you later."

They ate quickly and left—I heard them talking about going to The Circus, a nearby strip club—and I went on with my day, feeling a little giddy about the encounter. He was so handsome, with that dark skin and jet-black hair, and so polite. And on top of that he was a famous baseball player.

He called Hooters a couple of hours later and asked if I'd meet him at the Radisson hotel when I got off work. I didn't think that was a good idea, but I spoke to my housemate Cathleen and we decided there was strength in numbers.

When we got there, Jose was waiting for us with one of the other players. It was clear he wanted to hook him up with Cathleen, but that wasn't going to happen. Cathleen wasn't into the guy, and she said she wanted to leave. I honestly didn't feel right, either. I didn't like being in Jose's hotel room, and I felt icky in my greasy Hooters outfit. I have this thing about cleanliness. I feel better when I'm clean and pretty.

I told Jose that we were going to take off, assuming he'd make time for me if he was genuinely interested. He was disappointed, but he didn't get all pouty, like most guys do. He asked me if I'd have lunch with him the next day, and I said yes, so he told me to come by and pick him up before noon.

"You certainly handled that well," Cathleen told me on the way out.

"Have you ever seen a more beautiful man?" I asked her.

"He's not bad."

On the way to the hotel parking lot, I stopped to pick up a little rock that was lying next to the path.

"What's that for?" Cathleen asked.

"A memento from the night I met Jose Canseco," I said.

"You're crazy," she said, laughing.

"Maybe I'll get him to sign it," I said, only half-joking. I realized I was being a bit of a dork, but I was really attracted to him, and I felt that something good was about to happen.

I called my mom when I got home, still giddy, and told her all about Jose.

"Who?" she asked.

"Only like the most famous baseball player in the world!" I said. "He did that forty-forty thing."

"That's nice."

"He asked me to meet him for lunch tomorrow," I went on. "He's really cute."

"That sounds really exciting," she said. "Let me know how it goes."

I had a hard time falling asleep that night because I was thinking about my lunch date. The fact that Jose had noticed me when there were so many other pretty girls at Hooters made me feel special. I know it sounds silly, but I was young and not terribly worldly, and he seemed like a very sophisticated adult.

In the morning, my boyfriend, Steve, called to say hello and to see what I was up to, and I told him that Jose had come into the restaurant the previous day. He knew all about Jose, of course. He not only followed sports but also had one of those Sega video baseball games in which Jose was a featured player. "Did you talk to him?" he asked, and there was a little catch in his voice.

"Not really," I said. "Just to take his order and stuff."

I felt awful about lying to Steve, but I didn't think I should torture him unnecessarily. After all, nothing had happened. And in all likelihood nothing would happen. I was going to have lunch with the man, and I'd probably never see him again.

I took my time getting ready. I put on just the right amount of makeup, dressed in my geeky shorts and peach-colored Izod shirt, and drove to the hotel.

I parked in the Radisson lot and went up to his room, and it took him a while to answer. He opened the door, his eyes still cloudy with sleep, and invited me in.

"Oh, hey. Hi. What time is it?"

As I stepped through, he shut the door behind me and crawled back into bed. I was a little annoyed. I had expected him to be at least a little excited about our date, but here he was, still in his underwear, watching *The Price Is Right.* For a moment, I was reminded of my father, who spent a lot of time in front of the television in *his* underwear. But that's where the similarities ended.

"It's almost noon," I said.

"Why don't you come lay down with me for a few minutes?" he suggested.

"I thought we were going to lunch."

He took my hand and drew me onto the bed and tried to kiss me, but I was nervous and pulled away. He smiled, amused, and I managed to smile back. It *was* kind of funny: this big, huge tan guy in a rumpled bed watching a game show.

"What's so funny?" he asked, as I giggled.

"Nothing. I'm hungry."

"Okay, okay," he said and went to get ready.

I watched TV as I waited, trying to guess the prices of various everyday objects, and Jose appeared a few minutes later. He was wearing expensive slacks, a nice dress shirt, and plenty of jewelry.

I remember a Rolex watch and a sparkly bracelet. He went to the table and picked up his cell phone. This was back in the days before everyone had a cell phone, and I was impressed by that, too. I thought it was very glamorous.

We went downstairs and into the parking lot, and I remember watching this huge, handsome man squeeze into the passenger side of my little Honda CRX. He was twenty-eight years old. I was nineteen. I felt small and young and inexperienced, and for a moment I wondered what I was doing with him.

"You like Cleveland?" I asked.

"Not really. You?"

"I don't know it very well. I just come here for work."

I tried to make conversation on our way to the restaurant, but he didn't say much, and I thought maybe he was still tired, so I concentrated on the road. I didn't know my way around too well, and I practically broke into a sweat when I couldn't find the restaurant, but then I saw it halfway down the block and almost wept with relief. "There it is!" I said, as if we'd stumbled upon the holy grail.

"Yes it is," he said, and he looked at me funny, with this kind of half-grin, and made his eyebrows dance again.

We went inside and sat down, and I saw that people noticed us. *Him,* anyway. I realized that he really was pretty famous, and I thought I should try to do a little research on the guy before our next date—if there was a next date.

"So," he said, after we'd ordered. "You like working at Hooters?"

"It was only my third day," I said.

"Do you have a boyfriend?"

"No," I said. "Not really."

"What does that mean, *not really*?"

"Well, he lives in Ashland. And we hardly see each other anymore. And we've been sort of drifting apart anyway."

"What does he do?"

"He works at the college bookstore," I said. I guess Jose didn't realize that my boyfriend was still a kid like me. "He's a student."

The food arrived, and I was so nervous I could hardly eat. Under normal circumstances, I have a huge appetite, and I could have managed a big plate of steak and potatoes. But I had ordered a small, ladylike salad, and I could barely put a dent in that. Jose had no trouble scarfing down his sandwich, though. I noticed that, for a man his size, his hands were unusually small.

"So," I said. "Tell me about your marriage."

"I'm divorced," he said, as if that said it all, and he began to attack the second half of his fast-disappearing sandwich.

After lunch, he squeezed back into my car and asked me what I wanted to do. It was sort of a relief, to be honest. I thought he was going to ask me to drive back to the hotel and try to take me to bed, and I was so weak-kneed that I honestly didn't know if I'd be able to resist.

"I don't know," I said. "What do *you* want to do?"

"Is there a mall around here? Can we go to the mall?"

"Yes," I said.

"So, you got any brothers and sisters?" he asked.

"Yeah," I said. "I have a younger sister at home and an older sister in Boston."

He didn't say anything else. He just looked straight ahead at the road. I didn't say anything, either. I can talk to anyone, but around him I was completely tongue-tied.

We got to the mall and parked and started walking around, looking at the various stores, and before we'd gone very far people were coming over to ask for autographs. Jose signed one or two, but he wasn't comfortable with it, and he hurried me along to get away from the fans. I felt like such a geek next to him. He seemed so confident, and he looked like such an adult in his fancy clothes, and there I was, next to him, in my little shorts and my Keds. What a total nerd!

When we finally got away from the fans, he took me into the Calvin Klein store. "Let's look at some stuff," he said. For a moment, I felt kind of bad. I thought he must be ashamed of the way I looked and that he wanted to dress me up. But the feeling quickly passed. He kept pointing at items on the racks—dresses, slacks, nice shirts—and the fawning clerks hurried off to get them. I kept slipping in and out of the changing room, parading the various outfits in front of him, and I began to feel like a flesh-and-blood Barbie doll. It wasn't such a bad feeling.

"You know something?" Jose said at one point. "You have an amazing body."

The clerks kept bringing me stuff—a cashmere top, skirts, leggings—and Jose kept telling me that I looked great in everything.

"You really think so?" I asked.

"Yeah," he said. "Most women, you're going to see some flaws. But not you, Jessica. You are absolutely flawless."

Nobody had ever said anything so nice to me. It's a wonder I didn't swoon.

When he'd seen enough, he picked out one of the outfits—an elegant skirt with a matching top—and told me I should wear that instead of my shorts. I felt like a grown-up, almost transformed. In fact, I felt like a whole new person.

We walked toward the register, where he made me try on a few pairs of sunglasses. "There," he said, looking straight at me. "Those are perfect."

I thought he was going to buy me the outfit I was wearing and the sunglasses, but I was wrong. "We'll take all of it," he said.

It came to more than four thousand dollars.

I didn't know what to say. I kept thanking him and thanking him, and he kept telling me it was nothing, to not worry about it, and that he was glad to do it. And as we left the mall, with people staring at him and other people coming by to ask for autographs again, I suddenly felt like we were the perfect couple. Little Barbie had been remade, and she looked absolutely perfect next to her Latino hunk.

I drove him back to the Radisson, and he didn't invite me up. He had a game that night, and he had to leave for the ballpark shortly.

"I had a really amazing afternoon," I said. "I can't thank you enough for all of the beautiful things you bought me."

"It was nothing," he repeated.

I couldn't wait to get home to call my mother and tell her all about my day. I was so naive. I never stopped to think about the moral implications.

"Didn't you say you had a sister in Boston?" he asked, opening his door.

"Uh-huh."

"We're playing in Boston this weekend. Why don't you fly up and meet me there?"

"Seriously?"

"Sure. I'll have my assistant make arrangements."

"Wow." That's the best I could do: *Wow.*

"You want to come watch me play before we go?"

"I can't tonight. I'm working. How about tomorrow?"

"Okay."

"Can I bring my friend from work?"

"Sure," he said. "I'll have my assistant leave two tickets at Will Call."

He leaned over, gave me a little kiss, and lifted his huge, hulking frame out of the car. I watched him walk into the hotel and drove away.

When I got home, I ran inside with my Calvin Klein bags and boxes and called home.

"Oh my God, mom, you're not going to believe what he bought me. Dresses and cashmere and even these really cool sunglasses."

"He must be rich."

"He made them keep bringing me stuff. I thought he was going to buy me a pair of pants or something, but then he said, 'We'll take all of it.' And it came to over four thousand dollars!"

"Leave it to you to find a man like that!" my mother said, laughing.

"And he invited me to a game tomorrow night!"

"That's wonderful," she said. "Let me know how it goes."

My mother never made any judgments about anything or anyone, and at the time I used to think it was pretty great. Everything and anything I did was okay with her. But in the years to come, it began to bother me. I kind of wished I'd had better parenting. I'm not blaming my parents for the way I turned out, but I wish they'd given me a little more guidance. I wish they'd been a little more strict. It's not that my mom didn't care, but that she thought I was perfect.

I went to work that night, floating on air, and kept messing up everyone's orders. It didn't work against me. The patrons were as nice as ever.

The following night, May 26, 1993, wearing one of my brand-new outfits, which was probably a little too much for a baseball game, Cathleen and I drove to the game. The tickets were being held for us at the window, and we got good seats near the front. Jose looked cute in his Texas Rangers uniform. He saw me and waved and smiled. The people around us noticed. I tried not to gloat, but it was hard.

Then I looked around and saw a group of women in some seats near the diamond, even closer to the field. I figured those were the wives. A couple of them were looking in my direction, but they turned away when they saw me staring.

When the game finally got underway, I was totally shocked. I had never been to a baseball game, and it was arguably one of the most boring things I'd ever done in my life. Even the announcer sounded bored.

There was one bright moment, however. Jose was in the outfield, and Carlos Martinez of the Indians, the guy at bat, had whacked a good one right toward him. Jose looked like he was about to make a leaping catch, but the ball hit him on the head and bounced over the wall for a home run. I thought it was the funniest thing I'd ever seen, and I couldn't stop laughing.

After the game, Jose told me that had probably been the most embarrassing moment in his career, but he was able to laugh about it, too, which I found kind of endearing.

"I thought that's how the game was played," I joked. "You try to bounce the ball over the wall to get points for the other team."

He laughed and shook his head and told me to meet him back at the hotel. "I've got to deal with these assholes from the press," he said. "But I left a key for you at the front desk. Go on up to my room, and wait for me."

I dropped Cathleen off at her car and drove to the Radisson, excited. They had a key for me at the front desk, as promised, and the clerk looked at me kind of funny. It didn't fully register, though. I went up and sat on the bed and watched TV for about an hour, when he walked in.

"Hey," he said. "You hungry?"

"Yeah."

I thought we would go out, but he ordered room service. We had sandwiches and a couple of beers, and just as we were finishing his cell phone rang. He said hello and listened for a couple of seconds, then cupped his hand over the mouthpiece and told me he'd be right back. He stepped onto the balcony, shutting the door behind him, but I could still hear some of what he said. He was talking to his ex-wife, Esther, and I caught a few phrases here and there: "I miss you. . . . I'm just here on the road. . . . We're going to Boston this weekend, and I wish you'd come."

I was listening but trying not to listen, and it bothered me because it sounded like he was still in love with her. When he came back, he snapped out of it and moved the dishes off the bed and tried to kiss me.

"I don't even know you," I said.

"This is a good way to start," he said.

I let him kiss me—he was a real good kisser—and I even let him mess around with me a little. But the harder he tried, the more I fought him off. "I can't do this," I said.

"Why not?"

"I'm not a one-night stand type of person."

"Who said this was a one-night stand?"

"I've only ever had two boyfriends my whole life."

He kissed me again, but I pulled away when he tried to remove my clothes. "No," I said. "I mean it. I'm not doing this."

I kind of expected him to get mad, but he didn't. He smiled and kissed the top of my head. "Okay," he said.

"Will I see you tomorrow?" I asked.

"Why don't you spend the night?" he said.

"I told you already."

"Just to sleep," he said. "We don't have to do anything."

So I spent the night. And he didn't try anything. He actually stayed way over on his side of the big bed, which was kind of disappointing, since I wouldn't have minded cuddling a little. I was a little nervous, though. I kept waking up and looking at him, but he never even moved. He slept like a baby and snored real loud.

In the morning, he was up and dressed before I was even out of bed. He said he had to leave to go to the park, and he repeated what he'd said about his assistant and the travel arrangements for Boston. The team was leaving that night. He wanted me to fly the next day.

"Okay," I said.

He noticed the newspaper under the door, and he picked it up and turned to the sports pages. They had made a big deal about the way the ball had bounced off his head, and he seemed a little less amused than the night before. "Schmucks," he said.

"Who?" I asked.

"These reporters. They always make me out to be the bad guy of baseball." He opened the door and turned to face me. "Would you do me a favor?" he asked.

"What?"

"Can you pack my stuff for me?"

"Pack your stuff?"

"Yeah. Just put my things away and tidy up a little. That way I won't have to do it later."

"Okay," I said. I thought that was a little weird, but what did I know?

He took one of my hands in his and studied it for a moment. "And get your nails done," he said.

"Okay."

"Here." He handed me two hundred-dollar bills. "Get yourself a nice manicure."

"It costs that much?"

"I'll see you in Boston," he said and went off. I lay there for a minute, studying my nails. They looked like working-girl nails. I guess he wanted me to look a little more glamorous. Then I got his suitcase and started packing his things. It was really strange. I'm putting away his underwear and folding his fancy shirts and fancy slacks as if I were his wife or something. I thought back to the conversation he'd had the previous night with his ex-wife, and I wondered about that, too. I was increasingly confused, but I was also very attracted to him, so I decided I could live with a little confusion.

I drove home, called my mom, and told her he'd invited me to go to Boston and that I thought it would be fun because I'd get to see my sister Sam, who worked for a radio station there.

"Sounds exciting," she said. "But be careful. Don't have sex with him. And have fun with Sam. You guys call me, okay?"

I knew this was happening too fast, and I knew there was something wrong about having let him spend all that money on me, but I didn't have the sense to stop myself. And I didn't really want it to stop, so in that sense I was doubly to blame.

The weird thing is that I kind of wish my mother had tried to talk me out of going to Boston. I probably wouldn't have listened, but I may have reconsidered. Still, it wasn't her fault. As far as she was concerned, I could do no wrong. Maybe she really was excited for me.

Shortly after I got off the phone with her, Jose's assistant called with my travel information. I was suddenly more excited than ever.

Then I remembered that I was supposed to drive to Ashland that night to hang out with Steve and his best friend and his best friend's girlfriend, but for obvious reasons I didn't feel like going. I got into the tub and thought about calling Steve, but I didn't want to deal with it, so I called his best friend instead. "Listen," I said, "I'm not going to make it tonight. Do you mind telling Steve for me?"

"He's home. I just spoke to him. Why don't you tell him yourself?"

"I can't," I stammered. "I, uh—I met someone. But please don't say anything to Steve."

"Canseco?" he asked.

"How did you know?"

"Steve told me you said he'd come into the restaurant. He said he had a bad feeling about it."

I felt worse than ever. "Nothing happened with him," I said. "I just don't feel like driving to dinner tonight."

"Are you going to tell him?"

"Yes. I'll tell him I can't come to dinner. But please don't say anything about Jose yet."

"You're going to break his heart."

When I got off the phone, I called Steve and told him I couldn't come to dinner—I said I had to go to work—and got off the phone quickly. I didn't want to think about Steve. I wanted to think about Jose. I hardly knew the man, but I was already beginning to fall in love with him. And, if not him, at least the *idea* of him.

Meet the Family

Even as I got ready to fly to Boston, part of me knew that I wasn't prepared for a relationship with Jose Canseco. I wasn't prepared for a relationship with any adult, for that matter. I was just a kid, and not a particularly well-adjusted kid at that.

I was born Jessica Sekely in Pittsburgh, Pennsylvania, the second of three girls, but my father's business took the family to Ohio when I was still very young, and I grew up on a forty-two-acre farm in small-town Polk, a rural community near Ashland. My father's family is part Hungarian, and they lived in the Cleveland area. My mother's family was from Estes Park, Colorado, and Rapid City, South Dakota, and she is part American Indian.

When the weather was nice, my sisters and I spent our time outdoors. We'd ride bikes, run through cornfields, venture into unexplored corners of the property, and look for animals. We were always running into hedgehogs, woodchucks, skunks, and—closer to home—rabbits, and gobs of cats. I loved animals.

At dusk, we'd return to our 150-year-old farmhouse, do our chores, and sit down to dinner with Mom. Dad was seldom home in time to join us. He taught art at the Cleveland Institute of Art, and he had a small design business on the side, so his schedule was unpredictable. When he *was* around, however, he didn't seem to be present. He was distracted and self-absorbed, and we pretty much left him to himself. He ate when he wanted to eat, watched what he wanted to watch on TV, and came and left as he pleased.

Mom resented it—the man was practically a stranger—but she gradually came to accept it. After all, with the exception of providing for the family and paying the bills, his presence did nothing for her.

I think my parents were only happy in the very early years of their relationship, though I'm not even sure about that. They had met in a band. He played guitar and banjo, and she sang and also played guitar. By the time I was born, they were no longer making music together. For as long as I can remember, he slept on the couch downstairs, and she slept in the master bedroom upstairs.

The year I started kindergarten, my mom and my sister Rachel were in a terrible car accident. Both of them suffered head injuries, and my mother was actually in a coma for a week. When she finally came out of it, relatives thought we should give her time to recover. Samantha went to stay at my paternal grandmother's house, in Cleveland, and I went to stay nearby, with my aunt on my father's side. Rachel flew to Rapid City, South Dakota, where my mother's family nursed her back to health.

The three of us returned home late in the summer, and, for some strange reason, young as I was, I had a feeling that everything had changed. I was right. It was during this period, my mother later confided, that her marriage began to fall apart. Dad had only been there for her during the early years, she confirmed. And after the accident, when she needed him the most, he was more absent than ever.

I was too young to absorb everything that was going on, of course, but I remember some of it. Most pointedly, I remember feeling that my father was somehow inaccessible and that he was only *playing* at being a father. He would come through the front door, strip to his underwear, and park himself in front of the TV with his cigarettes. He seldom spoke to us, and then only in passing. He was in the house, but he was in his own world, and we were not part of it. This was the "absent" quality my mother had been complaining about for years, and eventually I began to see exactly what she meant. He seemed remarkably uninterested in the lives of his wife and three little girls. He came home to eat and sleep, a stocky, solid, disconnected man, lost to us, in a world of his own, simply passing through.

I can't remember a single, meaningful conversation I ever had with my father. And now that I think of it, I don't believe I ever heard him and my mother having a real conversation about anything substantial. I know it bothered her—she made this clear to me years later—but she also accepted it. *This is my life. This is the man I chose. It's my own fault.*

She was married to a man who had two distinct lives, a home life and a work life, and they didn't seem to intersect on any level. It would be many years before we discovered just how distinct and peculiar that other life was and that he had his reasons—reasons none of us could have ever imagined—for putting us in that old, antique, partially remodeled farmhouse, far from the city. But more on that later.

The fact is that in many respects my childhood was surprisingly normal. It wasn't marred by tragedy or abuse. Like every other kid, I loved my parents. I relied on them. I assumed that their parenting skills were on a par with the skills of the parents next door, and, indeed, with parents everywhere. It wasn't until many years later, when I was married and had a child of my own, that I finally began to think back to those early years and began to understand how my parents had shaped me, or, more specifically, failed to shape me.

In some ways, much as I hate to say it, my mother was as disconnected as my father. She made sure there was food in the house, certainly, and she kept the place clean. She got us to school on time, ran errands for us, bought us nice clothes, drove us from one extracurricular activity to the next, and was never less than 100 percent supportive. She had the time for it, certainly—her husband neither needed her nor wanted her—so she focused on us almost to a fault. Most damaging, perhaps, as she has admitted, she thought the three of us were absolutely perfect. As a result, there were no real boundaries in our home. No limits. No direction. My father neglected us; my mother loved us too much. There was no happy middle ground.

In most other respects, however, our lives were pretty good. We weren't privileged exactly, but we seemed to be better off than most of our neighbors. They were farmers, mostly, with rigid schedules and old-fashioned ways. My parents were artsy city types who didn't work the land and didn't mind if their three little girls ran around from daybreak till sunset.

There were many Amish people in the area, and I remember them as especially friendly. I felt sorry for the kids, though, in their dark, severe clothes and funny hats and bonnets. Some of them had to walk to school, even in bitterly cold weather, and sometimes we'd stop and pick them up, though everyone knew they were forbidden to ride in cars. Early on weekends we would find some of those same kids on our property, picking apples, and they would return late in the day with still-steaming pies. I think we got the better deal.

Still, at the end of the day, we remained outsiders to them and to everyone else, it seemed. We were slightly better off than the other townspeople, and it set us apart in ways I couldn't understand. I didn't feel lucky or special; I felt out of place, as if I didn't belong.

Finally, the summer after my mother's accident, when things at home began to take that subtle turn for the worse, I decided to plot my escape. I joined a gym class and dedicated myself to becoming an athlete. I went at it with all the fervor of a religious zealot. For the next five years, I was convinced I was going to become an Olympic gymnast, and my faith sustained me. The future looked bright. There was hope. Shortly after my tenth birthday, however, I had a change of heart. I told my mother I wanted to be a ballerina, and she enrolled me at the North Carolina School of the Arts, where I spent the next two summers. The following season I joined the Opus II Dance Studio and Tap Company, and, four or five times a week, my mother dutifully drove me to Ashland, Ohio.

"You're so beautiful," she would tell me. "You're so fancy." Sometimes her voice would crack with emotion, but I wasn't so sure those feelings had anything to do with me. She was very unhappy with my father and her life in general, and by this point she had finally begun to protest. The minute my father walked through the door, late as ever, she would begin to berate him, and the arguments would often continue long after I'd locked myself in my room. I drowned out their voices with a little help from Metallica.

My mother began to live vicariously through me, or so it appeared. I wasn't the smartest of my sisters by a long shot—I had ADD, and school was sheer torture—but I was the prettiest and most glamorous. Before long, I was auditioning for catalog work, and shortly thereafter I found myself modeling children's clothing. The first time I saw myself in a catalog, I thought for sure I'd become a model. I was only thirteen years old, but I imagined meeting people such as Arnold Schwarzenegger and Jean-Claude Van Damme. What can I say? Even then, I liked buff guys.

Eventually, I got tired of dancing. It was so regimented, and such hard work, and I began to feel that I was missing out on real life. Most kids hung out after school. Went to the Dairy Queen. Dances. Softball games. Bowling parties. I was slaving away at practice, preparing for recitals and putting on shows in and around Ashland, while they were off at *real* dances, having fun and enjoying life.

I began to suspect that a farm girl from Polk, Ohio, didn't have much chance of making it as a model and that maybe I should make an effort to have a normal life and be a normal kid.

By the time I got to Mapleton High School, I had turned into a very pretty young lady—albeit a flat-chested one—but the boys seemed to like me, and I liked them right back. At the age of fifteen, I discovered sex, or what I *thought* was sex. It was a very strange experience. The first time my first boyfriend, David, and I went to bed, I didn't understand why he had to hold his bobbing penis and maneuver it inside me; I had assumed it would find its way there on its own. Plus it hurt like hell. It was truly the most painful experience of my young life.

I used to sneak out of our farmhouse two or three nights a week, leaving pillows under the blanket just in case my mother looked in on me, then roll the car down the driveway and race over to his house. In the morning, just before dawn, I'd drive home, climb through the window, and get ready for school.

Later, I met Steve, my second boyfriend, and the sex was markedly better. I was really head over heels in love with Steve. He was a star basketball player at Ashland High, which was the cool school, and it was something of a miracle that he'd even look twice at me, a geek from Mapleton, albeit a pretty one. He was in love with me, too. And he was absolutely gorgeous! Six-foot-three, solid as a rock, with the most beautiful green eyes I'd ever seen.

Eventually, I practically moved in with him, and my mother didn't know what to do about it. She got no support from Dad and was worried about criticizing me, the perfect daughter, so I did as I pleased.

I think in many ways I simply wanted to get away from my parents. My mother veered from depression to angry screaming matches with my father, then back to depression again. My father ignored her and us, as he'd always done. I can honestly say—and it hurts me now, as I think back on it—that no one in my family ever said, "I love you." Not my father, not my mother, not my sisters. Those words were not part of the family vocabulary.

To make matters worse, at one point I was the only child at home. Samantha was away in college, and Rachel had gone to France as an exchange student. My mother only had me to talk to, and the talk was mostly about this miserable man she called her husband. I knew he was a miserable man just from the way she reacted to him. I didn't need her to point it out to me, especially with all that anger. There were times when her face was contorted by rage.

I loved her, and I felt loved by her, but I was tired of things at home. If she had just stopped to think about it, she may have understood why I was practically living at Steve's house. Our place was full of hate and rage and self-absorption. I wanted to have a normal family, and Steve's family became that family. I had Steve. I had his mom. I had home-cooked meals. We even played board games with his parents, and at the end of the evening we retired to our room and they retired to theirs. It was almost hard to believe: His parents slept in the same bed! That's the kind of family I wanted.

If they thought it strange that I was living under their roof with their son, they never mentioned it. Steve's mother enjoyed having me there. I made myself useful around the house, helped her clean up from time to time, and kept her company when the boys were out.

I came close to being unfaithful to Steve on only one occasion and that was the weekend Metallica played Cleveland. They were my favorite group, and Lars Ulrich was like a demigod to me. I was sixteen years old, and I just knew I had to meet him. I also knew that I had to go alone. If I went with friends, things would be unmanageable, and I'd never get a second chance at Lars. So I told my mother I was going with four friends, and I asked her if I could take the car.

"Well where is everyone?" she asked.

"I'm picking them up."

"Okay. But drive carefully. And don't get into trouble."

"Oh, mom!" I said and ran off while she was still talking.

I ended up in the nosebleed section, in the second to last row, but during the concert I managed to work my way down to the choice seats, and I finally parked myself right in front of the stage. I was so excited! I had every single Metallica album ever made, including many of their special collector's editions, and I knew half the lyrics by heart. Now here I was, in front of the stage, almost close enough to touch them, practically swooning with excitement.

Lars Ulrich spotted me and signaled to one of the security men, nodding, and the guy came over and handed me a backstage pass. The music was very loud, so I couldn't hear what he was saying, but I got the general idea. I guess that's the way it worked: If you were pretty, you had access.

When the show ended, I went backstage. The same security guard took me to Lars's dressing room, shutting the door behind me. Lars was grinning at me. "My," he said, "aren't you a pretty little girl?" I was completely tongue-tied. "Come here," he said, beckoning me over. "Why don't you give me a blow job real quick before we head over to the hotel."

I thought that was a little crude, and, for a moment there, I didn't really know what to do with myself. But suddenly the door swung open and in walked James Hetfield, the singer and rhythm guitarist. He looked from me, to Lars, back at me, and finally at Lars again. "What the hell is wrong with you, man?!" he asked, extremely pissed. "That girl's not even eighteen. I'm getting rid of her."

He had one of the security guards escort me to the door and walk me to my car, and I drove home, feeling pretty good about myself. In my muddled, adolescent mind, all that mattered was that Lars Ulrich thought I was pretty cute.

When my sister Rachel came home from France, I told her all about it. "I almost gave Lars Ulrich a blow job," I admitted.

"Wow," she said. "That is so cool!"

She was especially impressed by the way I'd been able to make my way from the nosebleed section to the stage to the inner sanctum, as if that were some kind of great accomplishment itself. Years later, as I remembered that moment, it made me realize that the absence of parenting in our home and the lack of moral guidance had been far more damaging than I'd imagined.

I never told Steve about my near miss with Lars Ulrich—I didn't want to open up that can of worms. I was still living primarily at his house, in his room, and making brief visits to my own home. But nothing there seemed to change, until one day my mother suddenly decided that she'd had enough. "I'm going back to school," she said. "I want to be a nurse."

This didn't happen overnight. Years later, my mother told me that she'd been seeing a therapist, in secret, to deal with the depression and anger. He had told her that she should try to do something productive with her life, that she was much too intelligent a woman to live through her children. They also talked about the possibility of divorce, but my mother didn't even want to broach the subject. Still, she wanted to take it one step at a time, and going off to school seemed like a good first step.

I was happy for her. Although she hadn't always been the most effective parent, I was glad to see my mother finally taking control of her life. She went off to study nursing, and I continued to muddle my way through what was left of high school.

Academically, my work left a lot to be desired. I had been diagnosed with ADD, as I said earlier, and I would read things without processing them. It was doubly frustrating because I had done the homework, but it didn't stick or compute. I scraped by with mostly C's, but my parents never once complained about my grades. Any other kid would have probably welcomed their indifference, and, at the time, I probably did, too. But I wish they would have cared more.

On the upside, I excelled at sports, especially track, and I was also a cheerleader, which made me popular among the jocks. This was important to me because I was kind of desperate for approval. I'm sure all of us are needy, but I was needier than most. Even little things went a long way, like the fact that—despite my tiny breasts—I was voted Best Body at the end of the school year.

When I graduated, I joined Steve at the Mansfield branch of Ohio State University. I would have liked to go to the main campus, but my grades weren't good enough, so I settled for the lesser school. On the plus side, neither Steve nor I had to leave home or do any growing up so things went on as before. I lived at his house five or six nights a week, and his parents continued to be everything my parents were not—delightful, attentive, happy, and full of life.

However, it was obvious—to me, anyway—that the relationship had reached some kind of plateau. It was all I had, however, and I wasn't about to give it up.

Whenever I went home to visit, once or twice a week, it only made me more aware of the shortcomings in my own family. My father still sat in front of the TV, saying nothing, and my mother was locked away in her room, studying for class. If Rachel or I made too much noise, or if Dad had the TV cranked up too loud, she'd burst out of the room, furious. "I am trying to study here!" she would yell. "Can't a person get a little consideration in this house?!"

Two months into college, I decided to drop out and transfer to Akron, hoping they would take me the following winter. In some ways, I was trying to force myself to become more independent. I didn't want to keep relying on the good graces of Steve and his family.

"I don't want you to leave," Steve said. "When are we going to see each other?"

"It's not that far," I said. "I'll come every weekend."

I think he felt me slipping away, and it frightened him. He was very happy in the relationship, and I think he probably imagined that we would get married someday and that maybe we'd just go on living with his mom and dad. It took him a long time to get used to the idea, and I had to jump through hoops to make him accept it.

My mother, however, thought it was a wonderful idea—everything I said or did struck her as absolutely wonderful—and she told me she would help me move to Akron when the time came.

"Just let me know what I can do for you, and when," she said, then locked herself in her room to study for her nursing finals.

There was one thing I desperately needed her help with, but I waited until the following January, when she graduated from nursing school with honors, before I even broached the subject. She was still giddy with excitement about her accomplishment, justifiably proud of herself, and we were alone in the house.

"Mom," I said. "Remember how you told me to ask you if I needed your help?"

"Sure. What is it?"

"I'd like bigger breasts."

I *did* want bigger breasts, and I wanted them very badly. I had a great body, but I'd been flat-chested all my life, just like my mother. And all my life I had heard her ridicule her own small breasts. Since I'd inherited those same small breasts from her, I was affected by what she said, and I had been thinking about doing something about it for a very long time.

She didn't like the idea, and at long last she began to act like a mother. It was silly. I was young. My breasts were absolutely perfect. I shouldn't subject my perfect little body to surgery.

I spent the next two months whining and begging, and she finally caved in. I knew she would. My mother wanted me to be happy, and I told her that I wouldn't be happy unless I had larger breasts.

In December 1992, I found a plastic surgeon in the Yellow Pages. My mother cosigned for my four thousand dollar loan, and on the appointed day she came with me to the hospital for the procedure. I was in pain for a few days, but I didn't mind. "Do you think they look nice?" I asked my mother.

"If you like them, I like them," she replied, but I could tell she felt lousy about the whole thing. I was a kid. I think she knew she should have stood her ground.

As for my father, he didn't even notice.

Now I had that loan hanging over me, which was costing me $117.30 every single month. "When you're up and about," my mother said, "you'll have to start paying off that loan."

The following month, I moved to Akron, Ohio, and took up residence in a house with four other girls. Me and my breasts were ready for a whole new life. I was going to study marketing and fashion merchandising, thinking that some day I might become a buyer for a big company. I also entertained the idea of becoming a veterinarian because I loved animals, but I knew that I would never be able to fulfill the academic requirements. The only A I ever got in college was in Lifeguarding, and that was probably because my new breasts looked so good in a bathing suit.

In any event, changing colleges didn't really change much. I had basically run from one campus to another, foolishly thinking that the change would change my life. I was also running away from Steve, looking to escape my dependence on him and his family, and I guess that was a good thing. But I felt lost and empty, and I began to fill the emptiness by going shopping. I liked nice clothes, and I liked expensive makeup. I know it seems shallow, and it was, but I don't think I was any more shallow than the next nineteen-year-old girl.

I kept shopping, never stopping to think of the consequences, and before long I was in horrible debt. My mother finally called me to discuss the situation. "You agreed to pay off your breasts, honey, remember? And now you seem to be having trouble making even the minimum payment on your credit card."

"I know, mom. What am I supposed to do?"

"Your father and I think you should get a job."

I don't know what shocked me more: the fact that she and Dad had actually spoken to each other and given some thought to my predicament or the idea that I was going to have to go to work.

"A job?" I repeated.

"It won't kill you."

She was right. It didn't kill me. But it came close.

Hooked

The conversation with my mother led to the job at Hooters, and the job, in turn, led to Jose Canseco. I'd gone to lunch with him, let him lavish me with gifts at the shopping mall, watched a ball ricochet off his head during a game against the Cleveland Indians, and was now on a plane, en route to our little rendezvous in Boston.

He was already out at Fenway Park when I arrived, so I took a cab to his hotel and found a key waiting for me at the front desk, as promised. I showered and got ready for him, and he arrived a little while later. He had a limo waiting downstairs, and we went off to a bar with some of his fellow players and a few wives and girlfriends.

Jose was incredibly attentive all evening, and for some strange reason this made me feel terrible. At one point, I went off to the ladies' room and started sobbing. One of the girls noticed that I seemed upset, and she followed me and tried to comfort me. I didn't even know her, but suddenly I was confessing everything. I had a boyfriend back in Ashland. I'd lied to him, and *worse*: I hadn't had the courage to tell him what I was doing. I didn't think I loved him anymore, but I had certainly loved him once, and I thought he deserved better than this. "If it wasn't over already, it's over now," I said, still sobbing. "I don't know what the hell I'm doing here. I don't even know what Jose wants from me. Is he just going to use me or what?"

The girl handed me some tissues, but she wasn't all that helpful. "You're going to have to do what you think is right," she said.

How would I know what was right? It seemed as if I'd coasted through life without any real awareness of right and wrong, or of what, exactly, constituted the difference.

When we returned to the table, I tried to act happy, and I drank too much too quickly. When we got back to the hotel, Jose could see that something was bothering me. "You want to tell me what's wrong?" he asked. I was surprised that he'd even noticed and even more surprised by his tenderness.

"I don't know," I said and began to cry. "I sort of have this boyfriend back home, and it's kind of over, but we never really ended it, officially. And I feel like the very least I can do is try to be honest with him, but instead of being honest, I'm sitting here in a hotel room, in Boston, with you—a guy I don't even know."

Jose had tears in his eyes. "I know exactly what you mean," he said. "I was with Esther for five years, married for four of them. She was the first big love of my life. I thought we would be together forever, and it was really hard for me when it didn't work out. I still miss her, and I still have feelings for her."

I couldn't believe he was being so honest with me, and it made me feel really close to him. The fact that he'd opened up about his ex-wife and that he'd admitted that he was still struggling with his feelings for her made me see him in a completely different light.

We went to bed but didn't make love. I'd had too much to drink, and I was feeling emotionally beaten, and he didn't push. Instead of cuddling, as I had hoped, he again retreated to his side of the bed. He seemed sad and distant, and I thought it must have had something to do with Esther. I wondered whether he was still in love with her, and whether he was asking himself what he was doing with me.

The next morning, we woke up late and went shopping at a Boston mall. He spent more than seven thousand dollars, buying me everything from a Louis Vuitton purse to a leather outfit by Versace. He was dressing me up, trying to transform his little farm girl into the kind of sophisticated lady he wanted on his arm. It made him happy, and it made me happy. Shopping is a wonderful antidepressant. For years afterward I depended on it to lift my spirits. It's amazing how quickly you forget your troubles when you're wandering from one store to another, spending your way into a good mood. In time, you even come to rely on it, often with financially disastrous results. But this was shopping at a whole new level. I had spent two thousand on each breast, and I had maxed out my only credit card, but Jose had managed to spend three times as much in the course of two visits to the mall.

We met my sister for lunch, and Jose went off to a game afterward. My sister thought he was a little arrogant, and I agreed, but I wrote it off as a cultural thing. Latino men were supposedly like that, and I found it kind of endearing. After lunch, my sister and I went off and found some Lee press-on nails for me—Jose had made another comment about them—and she hurried back to work. I returned to the hotel to get ready for my man.

I remember it was a Saturday—May 29, 1993. Jose had a day game. Boston creamed Texas. It got so bad that Jose actually came in to pitch the eighth inning, walking three, giving up two singles and three runs. The final score was 15–1.

Jose had always been telling everyone that he could pitch, and they'd never given him a chance. That afternoon they finally gave him a shot. Although he didn't do so well, he was happy about the whole experience. "How many guys can say they pitched a major-league game?" he told me later, while holding his elbow, which he seemed to have strained while pitching.

We got ready for a night on the town. I got dressed in a little black-and-white outfit he'd picked out for me, and I struggled with the press-on nails, which kept falling off.

"What the hell is that?" he asked, laughing. "Haven't you ever heard of a manicure?"

"I didn't know where to get one," I said.

He shook his head, still grinning. I guess he didn't realize what a kid I was.

We went out drinking again that night with some of the other players, and I made a conscious effort not to drink too much. I knew we were going to have sex later, and I was nervous.

When we got back to the hotel, we undressed and got into bed. I wanted to turn the lights off because I had only ever made love in the dark, but Jose wouldn't let me. "I want so see your beautiful body," he said.

I was shaking, but I'm not sure he noticed.

We kissed for a while, and I relaxed a little, but then I looked down and saw his wiener. It didn't look like any wiener I'd ever seen before. It was big and uncircumcised, and I thought it was one of the strangest things I'd ever seen. But as soon as it got hard, all the skin got pulled back and suddenly it looked pretty magnificent.

I honestly don't remember much about the sex. We made love in the standard, missionary position, and it was over. I was still thinking about his unusual penis. I'm from a farm town in middle America. We didn't get a lot of Latinos with uncircumcised wieners there. I also thought about his testicles. I hadn't had much experience with men, but it seemed to me that Jose's testicles were unusually small.

Afterward, as I lay there next to Jose, my mind racing, I started thinking about Steve. I felt more guilty than ever, and I realized that I needed to face him and tell him the truth. I did not make a habit of lying. I had never lied to Steve, and I don't think I had lied to my mother since that day I went to the Metallica concert. I didn't feel good about lying, which I felt was a plus—it meant I actually had some morals.

The only other sex-related thing I remember from that first trip came the following morning, when I asked Jose how many women he'd been with.

"Twelve or fifteen," he said.

I wondered what that meant. Were there three he wasn't sure about? Then he asked me how many men I'd been with.

"Two," I said. "With you, it's three."

He kissed me on the cheek. I think he liked that.

Jose walked me down to the lobby, put me in a cab to the airport, and left for his game.

On the flight back to Cleveland, I began to wonder whether I'd ever hear from Jose again. I liked him, and I was suddenly getting used to the idea of dating a man who was almost ten years older than me, but I wasn't sure he liked me back. I was also thinking about his ex-wife, Esther, and how he almost cried when he talked about her. I wondered if he was thinking of going back to her, and I got mad at myself for being so insecure. By the time the plane landed, I'd convinced myself that Jose was crazy about me and that we were going to get married and live happily ever after.

I got back to the house near campus, the one I shared with Cathleen and the other girls, and I walked through the door in a great mood. "I'm going to marry this man," I said. They didn't take it seriously, but they were very impressed with all the beautiful things Jose had bought me. I pulled them out of my suitcase, one at a time, and paraded around like a fashion model.

"So you really like this guy?" one of the girls asked me.

"He's amazing," I said, and I believed it. The whole Jose *experience* had been amazing. His Adonis-like looks. That first lunch. The way he kissed me. The shopping expeditions. I was even in awe that he had an assistant and with one call he could fly me to Boston. "This is the man I want to marry," I repeated.

Cathleen was very supportive, but I could see that the other girls thought I was dreaming. None of them spelled it out, but I knew what they were thinking: *Jose Canseco is a major-league ballplayer. He was only interested in getting laid. You'll never hear from him again.*

I went home, as if seeking reassurance, and told my mother

all about the trip to Boston. "He's only slept with about a dozen women," I said.

"That's not too bad," she said. "I mean, for a man of twenty-eight."

I also told her about his big, uncircumcised penis, in more detail than was absolutely necessary, and she listened politely. "Well," she said, "the Latin culture is very different. You'll see as you get to know him. But he sounds very interesting, and I'm glad you had a good time."

I still had to tell Steve, but I couldn't face him in person, so I phoned him instead. He asked me if I was coming over, and I told him no because I was still up in school and hadn't made it down and that I had to work that night. I couldn't believe I was lying to him again. I felt horrible.

"I have something to tell you," I said. There was a silence, and I heard Steve crying softly. "Steve?" I said.

"It's Jose Canseco, isn't it?"

I took a deep breath. "Yes," I said.

For a few moments neither of us said anything. Steve then told me he'd known all along. "That day you called to tell me you'd met him at the restaurant, my heart just sank. There was something in your voice, something about the way you told me about meeting him, and I just knew something was going to happen. Something bad."

He began to cry again. I felt awful. In some ways, we had both known the relationship was over, but Steve still had hopes for us, and I'd just crushed them. "I'm sorry," I said, even though I knew it wasn't enough. I had done a shitty thing to him. The right thing would have been to end the relationship first, and not to break the news about another man after the fact. "I'm really sorry."

Steve was crying harder now, and I felt so awful that I decided to go over to see him. At this point, I didn't care about getting caught in my little lie. This was more important. It was wrong of me not to be there for him, even if I was the one who was causing him all that pain—and especially because I was the one causing him pain.

When I got there, he became even more upset. "You don't get it, do you? That guy's just using you. He's way older than you. You shouldn't be with him. He's got a terrible reputation. I'm not just saying that. You read any sportswriter in the country, he'll tell you the same thing: *Canseco is a bad guy.*"

I didn't know what to say. I'd come over to try to comfort him, and I didn't feel like arguing. His mother walked into the living room. She was upset, too. "Jessica," she said. "You know how Steve feels about you, and how this whole family feels about you. You have no business dating a man like that. He's going to use you."

"No," I said. "He's really nice. He bought me all these nice clothes, and he was very respectful."

I didn't realize how pathetic that sounded. Plus it only served to make Steve more upset. An older guy was buying his girlfriend expensive clothes. How could he compete?

Steve's mom shook her head from side to side, visibly disappointed in me. "He's just using you," she repeated. "Don't you understand that?"

Actually, I didn't understand it. I didn't see it that way at all. They were the ones who didn't understand. This man really liked me. Why would he be flying me to Boston? Why would he be parading me around in front of his friends? He had even talked to me about his ex-wife and about all the pain he's endured during their divorce. I didn't care that he was older, and I didn't care what sportswriters around the country said about him. I knew better.

I went back to Akron and waited for him to call. And waited and waited. I thought about calling him, but I didn't know where he was, and it struck me that I didn't have his cell phone number. It was just as well. If he had just used me, I should start coming to terms with it.

It was June. The academic year was drawing to a close. I hadn't much liked school. I wondered what I was going to do with myself and whether I should just drop out. Then the phone rang. It was Jose. "I want you to meet me in Texas next week," he said.

"Okay," I said.

"I'll have my assistant call you."

I didn't hear from him for several days, and I began to panic. I called my mom, and she didn't know what to say, but I guess she was worried for me. "Maybe he's busy," she said. "Maybe something came up."

I felt really sad. I blamed myself for driving him away, and I kept going over everything we'd done together, trying to determine where I'd messed up. I never even thought to blame him. I never even considered the possibility that he was at fault. If he had lost interest, that was my fault, too.

I thought it was over. The relationship had ended before it had really begun.

I called my mom again, and she was even less helpful this time. "Maybe he found somebody else," she said.

"Thanks, Mom. That's exactly what I wanted to hear."

"Well, I'm sorry, dear, but you don't know him very well."

She was right about that. I decided to try to figure out who he was. I went to the college library and dug up all sorts of interesting information about him. I learned that Jose had done that forty-forty thing in 1988, when he was only twenty-three, and that the same year he was voted the American League's Most Valuable Player. I read that he'd been discovered in a Miami high school by the Oakland Athletics and that he was promoted to the majors in 1985. He got off to a shaky start, apparently, but he was still named Rookie of the Year, and he went on to prove himself quickly. He had back-to-back years with more than one hundred Runs Batted In, and he had three straight 30+ home run seasons. But after that big year, in 1988, he began to run into problems. He broke his hand in 1989 and missed the first half of the season, and he followed that up by getting into all sorts of trouble with the law. One time, he was clocked at 125 miles per hour in his Jaguar, and another time he was cited for having a loaded gun in his car.

Then the old Jose was back, hitting home runs out of the park. In the summer of 1990, he signed the most lucrative baseball contract in the history of the sport: $23.5 million for five years. I did the math. He was only halfway through the contract and was making close to $5 million a year. That worked out to about $400,000 a month. I didn't realize anyone could actually make that kind of money.

He continued to get in trouble with the police, though, mostly for speeding, and I read that he'd had an affair with Madonna, which I later asked him about and he denied. "It's those fucking asshole reporters. They just print what they want. I was never even attracted to her. She's not my type."

His image suffered. One time he almost got in a fistfight with a fan who'd been heckling him about Madonna, and the photos that appeared in the papers the next day didn't help. The fans began to boo when he went up to bat, even though he was still hitting plenty of home runs. I asked him about that, too. He said the media had turned everyone against him. They'd made him into the bad boy of baseball, and most people were dumb—they believed everything they read.

There was one other incident that bothered me more than the rest of the stories, and it dated back to early 1992, so it was pretty recent. Apparently, Jose and his ex-wife, Esther, got into a big fight one night in Miami, where he lived during the off-season. They were in separate cars—he was in a Porsche, and she was in a BMW—and they were racing down the street, side by side, screaming at each other through the open windows. Someone called the cops, and they were pulled over, but not before the cars collided. Jose was arrested and cited for domestic violence. I figured this was where the wife beating business came from, though there was no mention of any beating in any of the articles I saw.

I later asked Jose about this, too. He said it was total bullshit. He said the prosecutors had tried to get Esther to testify against him, expecting her to say that he had deliberately rammed her car, trying to kill her. But it wasn't true, and Esther refused to testify. Jose said that one incident more than any other damaged his reputation and really hurt him with the fans, that the media never went out of their way to correct any of the mistakes they had printed.

I didn't know what to believe, but I was worried. I began to think that maybe it was a good thing he hadn't bothered to get in touch, and of course that's when the phone rang. "I'm so sorry I didn't call," he said. "I've got family here in Texas with me. My father; my stepmother; my brother, Ozzie. It's been crazy. Get your sexy ass down here. Fly down tomorrow." He was very assertive. He knew what he wanted, and what he wanted was me.

I flew to Dallas the next morning. A limo picked me up at the airport and drove me to Colleyville, where he was living. I remember pulling up to this huge mansion and watching a giant turtle plod across the driveway. I got out of the limo and moved toward the door, and a smiling Jose opened it before I had the chance to ring the bell. He looked more Adonis-like than ever.

Two miniature schnauzers came out to greet me—more animals: This was a good sign—and Jose took me in his arms and kissed me.

"Glad you came," he said.

He brought me inside to meet the others, and I saw still more animals, a good sign: colorful birds, an iguana, two cats. *How bad can this guy be?* I thought. *He loves animals.*

Suddenly, his twin brother, Ozzie, popped into view. "Oh my God!" I said. "There are *two* of you?!"

Ozzie and Jose are fraternal twins, but they sure look a lot alike.

"I'm Ozzie," he said, shaking my hand. "Nice to meet you."

"Nice to meet you, too."

Then I met Vera, the Portuguese housekeeper, who was polite but a little distant, and a moment later we were in the family room, where Jose introduced me to his father and stepmother. They were very cordial and said all the right things. How nice it was to have me there; how much Jose had told them about me; that I should make myself at home, and so on.

I felt suddenly happy and optimistic. This hadn't turned out to be a one-night stand after all. Jose wouldn't be introducing me to his family unless our relationship was turning into something more serious.

Then it was time for lunch, so we went into the dining room, and Vera served us. It was kind of fancy. In my family, no one ever sat down to a meal, so I was a little intimidated. I was also starving, but I didn't want to look like a pig, so I just picked at the food. They spoke mostly English, but Jose's stepmother didn't have a great command of the language, so they spoke Spanish, too. I just smiled and tried to look pleasant and ladylike—I was wearing one of the outfits Jose had bought me—but I felt like I was way out of my league. I felt I had some growing up to do. I was a girl; Jose was looking for a woman.

After lunch, Jose said we should go to the pool. Before I changed, I snuck into the kitchen and stole a bagel and a bag of chips and took them with me into the bathroom. I scarfed them down while I changed into my bikini, but I was still hungry.

The pool was beautiful, with a plunging waterfall at one end. When I joined Jose in the water, he led me through the waterfall to the other side. There was a little cave back there. Jose pulled down my bikini bottom, and we had sex. It was quick and a little strange. When he was done, we swam back and he got out of the water and told me he had to go to the ballpark.

"Why don't you come out to the stadium in about an hour and watch?" he said. "Just bring one of the cars."

I showered, changed, and went downstairs, and Vera showed me in the direction of the garage. There were three cars in there: a Ferrari, a Lamborghini, and a Porsche. I found them a little intimidating. I went back to the kitchen to discuss it with Vera and decided the Porsche would be the least complicated of the three. I got in, started the engine, and pulled out. It was actually kind of fun, and I hadn't gone half a block when I found myself grinning. There was something seductive about the purr of a sports car's engine. For the first time in my life, I understood why men were so attracted to these little toys.

I hung out at the ballpark that night and found the game as boring as ever. Some of the Ranger wives and girlfriends were there, and they were nice enough—but not exactly friendly. Once again, I felt as if I were out of my league. I was a little nobody, an outsider. I got the impression they were taking bets on how long I'd survive.

Jose's family left the next day, so suddenly it was just the two of us in the house, with Vera and the menagerie. In the morning, Jose and I had sex again. It was unlike anything I was used to. He was forceful and aggressive, and he liked to bark orders as we went along. *Turn over. Faster. Lift up your hips. Let me see that ass.*

It was a little intimidating for someone as inexperienced as me, but I just went along with whatever he wanted. Steve had been young and docile and cuddly. We always made love at night, in the dark. Jose was experienced, aggressive, and knew what he wanted, and I thought I should try to learn from him. I wasn't enjoying it, exactly, but I was enjoying the fact that I was making him happy. He'd fuck me till he came, and then it was over. He wasn't bothered by the fact that I never came, and I certainly wasn't going to complain.

Not to jump ahead or anything, but I didn't have an orgasm with Jose for the next two years. If he noticed, he didn't care. We did what he wanted to do, when he wanted to do it. Doggy-style on the bed. On the bathroom floor. In the cave behind the waterfall. And I made myself like it because I could see that he was really into it. From time to time I even faked an orgasm, but I can't honestly say he noticed that, either.

One time he took me out in the Porsche, pulled off the side of the road, and told me to climb on top of him. I peeled off my underwear and turned to face him and lowered myself onto his penis, which was already hard. "Jesus," he said. "You have a great body. I love your body. I love your perfect tits."

That was enough for me. My man was wild about me, and he was happy. This was my job, to make him happy, to submit. I felt I had nothing to complain about. If I had felt strongly about not having an orgasm, I may have said something. But I said nothing, so Jose remained in the dark. I didn't know then that it was my job to speak up and that I should have been responsible for my own needs and happiness. When I look back on it, I realize it's easy to blame Jose, but it's also unfair. Jose didn't know there was a problem, so how could he be expected to fix it?

When we weren't fucking, and when Jose wasn't at the ballpark, we'd hang out by the pool, play with the animals, or watch TV. It was a lazy, languid existence. When he left for the ballpark, I'd lock myself in the room and masturbate. Then, sated, I'd go downstairs and ask Vera to fix me a little breakfast, and I'd laze away the afternoon on a deck chair by the pool.

Sometimes I'd nod off, with the miniature schnauzers curled up at my feet, and I remember waking up one day to find Jose moving toward me in his black bikini briefs. I thought I was dreaming. He was so gorgeous. I heard a splash and turned to see that the turtle had fallen into the pool, and—without missing a beat—Jose dove in to rescue it. He set it by the side of the pool, laughing, his teeth gleaming in the late-afternoon light. I was definitely in love.

I did have one complaint, though, and that was the fact that Jose didn't like to talk. No matter what I asked him, I'd get one-word answers or no answers at all. He was emotionally shut down, but once again I blamed myself. Maybe he didn't feel comfortable with me yet. Maybe he wasn't ready for that kind of intimacy. Maybe he was waiting to see where the relationship went before baring his soul. It was up to me to be there for him when he was ready to open up.

But he didn't open up. He was always quiet, always monosyllabic, always the same Jose. The only one time I'd even glimpsed a different side of him had been earlier in the week, when his father was around. I can't say I liked his father. He was disrespectful and dismissive of Jose, and Jose didn't react to it. If anything, he seemed to regress. I remember one time they exchanged harsh words in Spanish, and I looked up to see Jose's face transformed into the face of the lost little boy he had once been.

"What's the story between you and your father?" I asked him later.

"Nothing," he said. "My dad's a control freak. I just ignore him."

It would be a long time before I was able to pull the story out of him, and, when I did, it made me feel closer to him than ever. It had not been a happy childhood. Jose and Ozzie had always been made to feel like they would never amount to anything. "You and your brother are a pair of losers," his father would say repeatedly. "You are a terrible disappointment to me. You're going to end up behind the counter at McDonald's."

I didn't understand why Jose bothered putting up with him. He was living out the American dream, and he was rich beyond anything he had ever imagined; yet, he invited the old man into his house and let him criticize him at every turn. The way he had handled a particular play. His attitude toward the press. Even his carelessness with money. It was a mystery to me. If I had been in Jose's shoes, I would have kicked the old man out and told him never to come back. But it's never as simple or as easy as it looks. I had issues with my own parents, and I'd been damaged in ways I hadn't yet begun to understand, and I remained as connected to them as Jose was to his disapproving, mean-hearted father. A lot of parents don't realize how much they influence the lives of their children or the levels of damage they can inflict.

I was pretty damaged myself. I began to realize that Jose was as absent as my father, but I accepted it. I would ask him about his day, the game, his cars, his friends, his ex-wife, and his answers were always: *Good. Okay. Fine.* And he never once asked me about me. He didn't ask about school. He didn't ask about my family. He didn't ask about my hopes and dreams. In retrospect, I see that it was a form of emotional abuse and not dissimilar from the abuse I'd suffered at home. The absence, the neglect, the self-absorption. In a brief moment of clarity, I remember feeling as if I were reliving my childhood, and I couldn't for the life of me understand why. Did I think I would get it right this time around? That I could fix it?

Then again, I got tired of overanalyzing everything. If I was bothered by Jose's self-involvement, the less-than-gratifying sex, the lack of communication, and the complete absence of intimacy, there were other things that made up for them. The *physical* Jose, for one: that indescribably gorgeous man next to me in bed. And there were limitless perks. Fast cars. Lunch by the pool. Round-the-clock service. Shopping expeditions. Everything seemed designed to make life as easy and effortless as possible, and it worked. Would you have complained? I certainly didn't. I was a shallow, happy girl. I ate when I was told to eat. I showed up at the ballpark as ordered. And when I was told to get on my hands and knees on the edge of the bed, I did it with a pleasant smile. In short, I did what plenty of damaged women had done before me and will probably continue to do until the end of time: I fell more deeply in love with him with every passing day.

4

CHAPTER

Unfaithfully Mine

By the time I got back to Akron in July of 1993, I was convinced that I was going to marry Jose. I couldn't stop talking about him. I bored my housemates silly. I bored my mother. I bored my sisters.

School was out for the summer, but Cathleen and I were still working at Hooters. One afternoon, as I was boring her with yet another story about Jose, I happened to mention that his permanent, off-season home was in Miami.

"Miami?" she said. "Really? I've been thinking about moving to Florida. I was in Orlando years ago, and I really liked it. And I'm just sick and tired of school and of the cold weather."

One of the managers overheard us talking and joined the conversation. "You girls would do great in Florida," he said. "The Hooters there are big moneymakers."

In a matter of days, we had decided to transfer to the University of Central Florida, in Orlando, and made plans to drive down together. I called my mother to break the news. "I'm moving to Orlando," I said.

"Really?" she asked. "Is that what you want to do?"

"Yes. I think it will be fun down there."

"Well, I want you to be happy, and I don't want to stand in

your way, but please think about it before you make up your mind."

"I've already thought about it," I said. "I'm moving."

I then called Jose to tell him about our plans, noting that both Cathleen and I were sick of school and sick of the endless Ohio winters. "Orlando is good," he said. "You'll be close to my place in Miami."

I told myself that the move had nothing to do with Jose, and I'd like to believe it, but I know it isn't entirely true. Moving to Florida had been Cathleen's idea, yes, but I wouldn't have gone along with it so readily if I hadn't had hopes for me and Jose.

A few days later, I packed my Louis Vuitton bag, picked up the cat, grabbed a plant, climbed into the passenger seat of Cathleen's Geo Metro, and we hit the road.

When we arrived, everything seemed effortless. We found an apartment and settled in. The weather was nice, and the people were pleasant and unrushed. I picked up the local paper and read about bikini contests, a local custom, and tried my luck. That turned out to be as effortless as everything else in Orlando. I would arrive at a given bar, wait for my turn like a good little girl, then parade across a small stage in my very small bikini. The men would hoot and holler, I would smile pleasantly, and when the show was over, I'd go home with two hundred dollars in cash. I entered three bikini contests that first week, and—not to brag or anything—I won them all. There were plenty of wet T-shirt contests, too, and I was tempted, but I wasn't quite *that* liberal.

Cathleen went to work for Hooters. She made great tips. Life was good. We more than managed. I called Jose in Texas to give him my new number and to hint that I was ready to visit again at a moment's notice. I caught him in a lousy mood. His arm hadn't recovered from his pitching in the game against the Red Sox at the end of May. It was beginning to look like he might need surgery.

"I'll call you when I know what's going on," he said.

A few days later, in the middle of our second week in Orlando, the phone rang. I was sure it was Jose, but it was Cathleen's mom. Cathleen had failed to tell her parents that she was moving to Orlando, and they'd only just found out through one of our housemates. Her father got on the phone. He was a real parent, and he was livid. "You get your ass back here right away, you hear me?!"

She heard. As we began packing up for the trip home, Jose called. "I have to fly to Los Angeles for surgery, then I'm going back to Texas to recuperate," he said.

"Is it bad?"

"I don't think so," he said. "I just messed up some ligaments in my right arm."

"You want me to go with you?"

"No, but I want you to meet me back in Colleyville."

I explained that Orlando hadn't worked out, and that Cathleen and I were heading back to Ohio, so he made arrangements to fly me in from Cleveland. Cathleen and I drove home in sharply contrasting moods. She was going home to deal with her angry parents, and I was thrilled about hooking up with my man.

When I landed in Texas, there was another limo waiting for me. We drove to the house and Jose greeted me at the front door, his arm bandaged and in a sling. I had brought him a huge stuffed dinosaur, and he laughed and hugged me and told me it was nice to see me. For a moment, he acted like a real boyfriend. But by the time I'd unpacked and come down for dinner, he was in a lousy mood. His arm hurt, and he was fed up with all the assholes in baseball.

He still had to go to the park every day, but because he was injured they didn't work him out as hard, and he was around more often. He'd come out to the pool in his black briefs, with his arm in a sling, and my heart would still jump every single time. I thought we'd get a chance to talk more and grow closer, but all he did was grumble. He seemed more preoccupied than usual. He had a pager—it would beep, and he would call in for messages—and it kept going off.

"Who's calling you all the time?" I asked.

"It's nothing. It's the guys."

The next time his pager went off, I was in the bathroom when he phoned to get his message. He took the call on speakerphone not knowing I was there, and I heard the operator reading the message back to him. "Lucy says she will be there at two." I felt ill. Who was Lucy? Where was she going to be at two?

An hour later, shortly after noon, Jose said he had to go to the ballpark. I didn't say anything. Maybe Lucy was a secretary. Maybe she was his lawyer. Maybe she was part of some endorsement deal. I didn't want to screw anything up between us.

In the course of the next few days, the beeper kept going off, and Jose kept disappearing. One day he took a shower *before* he went to the ballpark. This made no sense at all. Jose wasn't big on showers, and I knew he wasn't getting clean and pretty for the other players. But I still said nothing.

He came in late that night, dropped onto his side of the bed—he never cuddled—and promptly fell asleep. When I heard his steady, rhythmic breathing, I got out of bed, locked myself in the bathroom, and wept. I stifled my sobs with a towel. I didn't want to wake him. I didn't want him to know I was unhappy.

The following morning, to my great surprise, he noticed that I wasn't my usual chipper self. "What's wrong?" he asked. The question surprised me. He never asked me anything about me, and I was used to it by now. Life revolved around Jose.

"Nothing," I lied. "I didn't sleep well."

"Want to go shopping?"

"Sure," I said and felt better.

We went to the mall. I came home with shoes, silk shirts, two purses, and a bracelet. Like I said, shopping is a wonderful antidepressant.

As for Jose's pager, it remained a large part of our lives. It would buzz, and he'd go off to make a call behind closed doors, and he'd disappear for a few hours. I didn't want to believe that he was seeing Lucy or anybody else. I knew that something was wrong and that I didn't want to live like that, with that kind of uncertainty, but by then I guess I was already addicted to Jose. I wish I could explain why, exactly, but it's difficult. It makes me feel lousy about myself when I think about it. He was beautiful, and he bought me beautiful things, and I had Vera there to take care of all my needs, but was I really so easily satisfied? To this day, I can't explain it. Then again, it's hard to be logical about emotions, and I guess that's what makes life so confusing.

One day, I answered the house phone—it was ringing, and it seemed like the logical thing to do—and a woman said his name, sounding startled, then quickly hung up. Jose came out into the hallway, his brow furrowed. "Who was that?"

"I don't know," I said. "Some woman."

"Don't answer the phones anymore," he snapped. "You understand?" Then he stormed into the kitchen, and I heard him hollering at Vera in Spanish. The only word I recognized was *teléfono.*

I didn't confront him about this. When I think back on it, it occurs to me that Jose and I hardly ever talked about anything. It's hard to believe that we were together in that house for hours on end, sometimes for days at a time, and we still had nothing of note to say to each other. "Where's the iguana?" "There's too much chlorine in the pool." "I'm going to fire the gardener." "You hungry?"

We'd have sex in the cave, on the dining room table, with me draped over the couch, and—from time to time—in bed. Then we'd watch a little TV and go to sleep.

One night, just as he was about to put out the light, the phone rang. He picked it up. It was Esther, and I guess he was too tired to take the call behind closed doors.

"I'm getting ready for bed," he said.

"Tell me you love me," she said. Her voice was faint, but clear. "Tell me you love me, Jose."

"I love you," Jose said.

I felt like he'd just stuck a knife into my chest. I was dizzy, the blood was pounding in my ears, and I didn't hear the rest of the brief conversation.

"Jessica!"

"What?" I turned to look at Jose, startled, as if coming out of a trance.

"Did you hear what I said?"

"No," I said. "What?"

"That was Esther. She just does that. I had to tell her that, or I couldn't get her off the phone. It doesn't mean anything."

"Are you sure you don't love her?"

"Of course I'm sure!"

"Maybe she does that to make sure there's no one in bed with you."

"Maybe. How the hell should I know? And who cares?"

"I'm in the room with you. Am I nobody?"

"Jesus! What the fuck are we arguing for?! I told you it was nothing."

He turned out the light, turned his back to me, and went to sleep. I sat there, not moving, until he fell asleep. Then I went into the bathroom and wept.

The next morning, he left early. I went downstairs to have breakfast, and the phone rang. I went to reach for it but Vera stopped me.

"No, Jessica," she said. "Mr. Canseco doesn't want that."

"Who are all these other women, Vera? Where does he keep going all the time?"

I was near tears, and I guess Vera felt sorry for me. She began to tell me a little about Jose. Yes, she said, there were other girls.

That was just the way Jose was. She told me there had been another girl staying at the house with him when I first came to visit him in Texas, a girl who I'll call Diane, and that she had left the morning I arrived.

"You mean, when his parents and his brother were here?"

"Yes," she said, nodding glumly.

"That's why he didn't call to invite me down?"

"*Si.*"

"So one girl leaves, and I arrive to take her place, and nobody seems to have a problem with it?"

She shrugged. She didn't question such things. Jose was Jose, and the family was the family. If they had a problem with Jose's morality, or lack of it, they certainly weren't discussing it with her.

Vera could see that I was becoming increasingly upset, and she tried to make me feel better. "It is different with you," she said. "You are special."

"How do you know?"

"I can just tell. He cares about you."

I don't know why I believed her, but I know I wanted to believe her. I also wanted to know more about these other girls. It was pretty obvious that Jose had slept with a lot more than "twelve or fifteen" women.

"They're just girls," Vera said. "They don't mean anything to him."

"I want to know, Vera."

"I'm sorry," she said, shaking her head from side to side. "I can't talk bad about Mr. Canseco. But please don't think about it anymore. I like you, Jessica. And I know he likes you, too."

"I promise I won't say anything."

"No. You should be smart about this. I think you're the one."

That made me feel much better, despite the fact that Vera couldn't possibly know whether I was *the one*. But an hour later, I was depressed again. I called my mother and told her about the other girls, about that damn pager, and about the I-love-you conversation he'd had with his ex-wife.

"Maybe you should come home," she said.

I didn't know what to do. I was alone most of the time, with Vera, the animals, and the TV. And when Jose was around, he had nothing to say. I thought my mother was right—here she was, finally offering me solid guidance—so I said the only thing I could think of saying. "Vera thinks I'm the one."

"Who?"

"Vera. The housekeeper."

"She does?"

"She says he really likes me. She says I'm not like the other girls."

"I don't know what you want me to say, honey."

"I'll be okay, mom. Thanks for listening."

When Jose came home, I didn't want to say anything because I didn't want to betray Vera. I tried to talk about other things—his day at the park, his early years in Cuba, his mother who had died of cancer when he was nineteen—but he either ignored my questions entirely or said he didn't feel like talking. That was one of Jose's favorite lines: "I don't feel like talking right now." It was a polite way of telling me to leave him the hell alone. He *never* felt like talking.

The next day he took me shopping again, and the day after that he told me to come out to the park, early, and to wear some of the pretty things he had just bought me. I showed up looking like a million bucks, and the other players noticed. Jose was beaming. I was there for show. He had dressed me up to show me off. *That girl there belongs to me.* If I didn't see it then, I see it now: Everything was for show. Me. The cars. The nice clothes. Everything was about Jose, to shed light on Jose, to make Jose look good.

I guess a small part of me *was* aware of it, however, because I remember standing there, like an ornament, being ogled by the other players, and thinking that I missed Steve. I missed cuddling with him. I missed talking to him. I missed being myself. Then the feeling passed, and I realized I was kidding myself. It had been over with Steve long before it ended. *Jose was terrific,* I told myself. If it wasn't working, it was my fault.

I started spending more time at the ballpark, hanging out with the other players' wives and girlfriends. I thought maybe I could pick up a few pointers from them. They were nice to me, but I got the impression that I was still very much an outsider. They seemed so much more sophisticated than I was, and they seemed far more accustomed to the rhythms of being good wives and good girlfriends. Oddly, they didn't talk much about the guys. They talked about shopping and cars and they showed off their baubles. I thought they were just being cautious around me, that I wasn't officially part of their little club yet, and that they were just waiting to see whether Jose was going to keep me. I decided to be patient. I could talk about clothes and cars with the best of them.

Sometimes, we'd go to lunch together, in our perfect little outfits, with our chic little purses, and Jose didn't like it. The third time I went to lunch with a few of the wives, he took me aside later and told me to stop seeing them. "Those girls are bad girls," he said. "They cheat on their husbands. And they're liars."

Jose was only concerned about what I might learn about him, even if the chances of my learning anything were next to nil. I didn't find out until much later that baseball wives have their own code and that one of the tenets is to not talk about anything of substance. At that point in my relationship with Jose, I was still auditioning to become a member of the club, and—as an outsider—I wasn't covered by the same rules. I think Jose was worried that they might actually tell me ugly things about him.

"Why don't you get a membership at the gym?" he suggested one afternoon.

"I thought you liked having me at the ballpark?"

"I do like you at the park," he said. "But I don't like those women. They're liars."

"All they talk about is clothes and stuff. What are they going to lie about? How much they paid for a dress?"

"Just take a break from them," he snapped. "If you don't want to go to the gym, I'll see you when I get home."

I did what he told me to do, docile as ever. I figured it was some kind of Latino thing. A good girl does what her man tells her to do. Above all else, I wanted to be a good girl. If I was a good girl, I might become the official girlfriend. And if I became the girlfriend, maybe I'd become the wife.

I honestly don't know why I was so eager to get married. I was now all of twenty years old, and I imagine I was looking for a home and sanctuary. I thought that's what all girls wanted. I thought the goal was to find a man to take care of you, and in my mind I'd already found him.

So why was I locking myself up in the bathroom night after night sobbing?

I decided I needed some distance from Jose, to try to get my head clear. When he wasn't around, I almost felt normal. But the moment he returned to the house, I was hooked again. Maybe that's what it's like for an alcoholic. If he's busy working or playing, he doesn't think about liquor. But let him drive past a flashing neon sign outside a bar, and it's all he can do to keep driving.

"I think I'm going to go home for a few days to visit my family," I told him one morning.

"Okay," he said.

That was it? *Okay?!* Couldn't he have protested a little? Couldn't he have told me not to go? That he would miss me too much?

"You don't mind?" I asked, giving him a chance to reconsider. I felt suddenly horribly insecure. I felt as if he were looking forward to a break from me.

"No," he said. "It'll probably be good for you."

As I packed for the flight home, I wondered whether Jose was tired of me. I was sure there'd be someone on my side of the bed before the plane had even landed in Cleveland. I wondered if he'd cuddle with her, and whether he didn't cuddle with me because, deep down, he knew I wasn't the one for him.

I was driving myself crazy.

Jose drove me to the airport. He kissed me good-bye. He didn't say he loved me. I didn't say I loved him, either. I wanted to, but I didn't want to put him on the spot. How pathetic is that?

I stayed with my parents. My mom and I talked a little about Jose before she went to work. I don't remember seeing much of my father. I was in bed by the time he got home, and he was gone by the time I got up.

I thought about going to see Steve, but I knew I'd only feel bad about the way I'd broken things off and that he'd probably be less than thrilled to see me. Plus, I didn't particularly want to find out whether he was already seeing someone else.

During that fall I went to visit Cathleen and even spent a few nights at her place just to get away from my family. She was back at the Cleveland Hooters, still dreaming of moving to Florida, and it looked like her parents were slowly getting used to the idea.

Jose called from time to time, and I called him, too. Every time I called, though, I thought about the pager, how it had buzzed all day, and that just made me sad. And whenever I reached him, we always had the same non-conversations. *Hey, how are you? Cold up in Ohio? You doing anything fun?* Never has so little been said about absolutely nothing.

One afternoon, inspired by the old neighborhood, I put on a pair of jogging shoes and began to run. I felt like I had in the old days, back when I was on the track team in high school, and I realized that exercise was almost as effective an antidepressant as shopping.

I took a couple of shifts at Hooters and discovered that Cleveland had its own bikini contests. I was on stage two days later, winning, and I went back for another victory lap a few days after that. It was a living. A *lousy* living, sure, but it paid some bills.

Three weeks into my little vacation, I realized I really missed Jose. I didn't want to wait on tables. I didn't want to parade around in a little bikini in front of a hundred horny, hooting men. And I didn't want to go back to school because I couldn't retain much of what I read.

I began to misremember my time with Jose. I forgot about the late-night call from his ex-wife. I forgot about that endlessly buzzing pager. I even forgot about the nights I had locked myself in the bathroom, burying my sobs in a towel so I wouldn't wake him.

I began to think that there was nothing wrong with fast cars, nice clothes, and a big house where someone tended to my every need. I missed sitting by the pool, eating lunch on a tray, and watching the cats tease the poor turtle as it plodded across the yard.

Maybe happiness consisted in making Jose happy. If I worked harder and made Jose truly happy, the pager would stop buzzing. Right?

I wanted to save myself from my unpromising life. Other

people got up in the morning to face dead-end jobs, and they would go to bed every night unfulfilled and miserable, but I didn't want to be one of those people. Jose lived the fairy tale. And even if he did have the starring role, my part wasn't all that bad.

Cathleen arrived at work one afternoon, beaming, and made an announcement that ultimately clinched my decision. "I'm going," she said.

"Where?"

"To Orlando. My parents are finally cool with it. I'm transferring to UCF."

"Wow. How'd you convince them?"

"I screamed and cried."

"When are you leaving?" I asked.

"As soon as I can pack. You want to come?"

"Yes!" I said. I didn't even have to think about it. Anything was better than Ohio. There was nothing for me in Ohio. And Orlando was closer to Miami.

The following day, I called Jose and told him I was moving to Orlando.

"Why don't you come down to Miami?"

I almost wept with happiness, which says a little something about my disordered state of mind.

"Okay," I said, but then I remembered my commitment to Cathleen. "I almost forgot! I'm supposed to be moving with Cathleen."

"Just bring all your stuff," he replied. "When you're ready to visit Orlando, you can take one of the cars."

"You sure?"

"Absolutely," he said.

"I've missed you," I managed.

"I'll have my assistant call you with the travel arrangements," he said and hung up.

Love and Steroids

Two days later, I flew to Miami wearing a floral palazzo outfit, thinking I looked very cool. Jose was waiting for me at the airport, a very promising sign, looking as gorgeous and irresistible as ever. He grinned when he saw me coming.

"Hey, baby," he said, giving me a big hug and kiss. "How are you? You look great."

We picked up my suitcases—all four of them—and drove out to his house in the Cocoplum section of Miami, a very nice part of town. The house was at the top of a hill, and huge, and it put the ranch-style place in Colleyville to shame. It was very dramatic, too, part Art Deco, part modern, and it seemed to go on forever.

Jose and I got out of the car and crossed to the front door. He led me inside, and I was astonished by the size of the place, if less so by the decor. It had cathedral ceilings, and everything was painted pink. There were pink and yellow triangles on the walls, huge, showy chandeliers, and all sorts of Asian art—paintings, sculptures, framed ornaments, and immense vases. I found out later that Jose's ex-wife had been responsible for the interior design. It was immediately apparent that our tastes were quite different. I wasn't all that sophisticated myself—floral palazzo!—but I knew I could do better than this.

Vera came out to greet me, followed by the cats, and I saw the familiar turtle out back, still plodding along, going nowhere slowly, except he'd been shipped to his rightful, off-season home. There was a pool and a dock. The house was right on the canal, and Jose had two boats moored to it: a fishing boat and a fifty-two-foot Hatteras.

"You like it?" he asked, gesturing vaguely toward the house.

"It's very nice," I said.

"Why don't you settle in?" he said. "Ozzie's coming by later with his girlfriend. We're going out to dinner."

He and Vera helped me take the suitcases upstairs, and I noticed there were mirrors all around the bed. I tried not to think about it and went off to unpack. I felt like a wife, returning from a trip. I was nervous, but kind of excited, too. Then Jose came up and plopped down on the bed and watched me unpack.

When I was done, I showered, dressed, and changed into one of my Calvin Klein outfits, and by the time I got downstairs Ozzie and his girlfriend, whom I'll call Lorraine, had arrived. One of Lorraine's girlfriends had come with them, and it seemed to me that she and Lorraine looked very glamorous, with their fancy dresses and all that makeup and their hair done to perfection. I felt like a farm girl who was trying to look chic in her little Calvin Klein outfit and not quite pulling it off. They were very nice, though. They looked me up and down and didn't say anything mean, and we all went off to dinner.

We ended up at some expensive sushi place in Miami. I'd never had sushi in my life, so maybe I *was* a total farm girl. I hated it. I kept pretending to eat it, and at one point, when Ozzie was looking at me, I actually had to put a slab of raw fish in my mouth. I excused myself a little later and hurried to the ladies' room and promptly spat it out. When I returned, still smiling, they were attacking another huge plate of dead fish. They kept going on and on about how wonderful it was, like they were practically coming or something.

Jose didn't even notice my discomfort. It would have been nice if I could have said something to him, and perhaps ordered something off the menu—something cooked—but he didn't ask. When we got home, I raided the fridge and pantry and stuffed my face. At that point, a burger from the Dairy Queen sounded like heaven.

We went back for sushi the next night, and I suffered in silence. There I was, the meek, submissive girlfriend, intent on not making waves. I didn't want to bother anyone. I wanted to be liked. I wanted to be one of the gang. So I kept my mouth shut and smiled and pretended to have a good time.

Jose and I had sex two or three times a day. I still didn't have an orgasm, but now I could see myself in the mirror not having an orgasm. One time, while Jose was taking me from behind, I turned my head and saw him back there, parked between my legs, thrusting in and out, and watching himself in the mirror. It was pretty strange. The man really loved himself. I wondered what his secret was. I could have used a little self-love myself. In those days, I didn't like myself very much at all.

During the day, Jose had nowhere to go, so we lounged around, not making conversation. Our conversations were about as gratifying as our sex life. He'd make calls and speak to his friends and his family, and whenever I asked who he was talking to, he'd always say the same thing: "Nobody." There were a lot of nobodies in his life.

Then the damn pager started up again. Buzz, buzz, buzz. Vibrating away on the foyer table. One time, I was in the kitchen, looking to steal some food, and I heard him call in and give the operator his code. I made a mental note of it. The next time Jose went out, I called in for messages. I gave the operator Jose's code, and she read the messages to me, one at a time. There had been eight or nine calls in the space of one afternoon, all of them from women, and some of them were alarmingly specific: "I'll see you at my place at four." "I'll be by the pool." "Try to be on time this time." Most of the women also used endearments: *Honey. Baby. Amorcito mio.*

I was crushed. I didn't say anything to Jose, but I told him that I was going to visit Cathleen in Orlando to help her figure out the apartment situation. We were sharing a place, ostensibly, and I didn't want to leave her in the lurch.

Jose asked me to take the Suburban, which was about four times the size of my Honda CRX, and when I was climbing behind the wheel, I hit something with my ankle. I looked down. There had been a tape recorder stuck to the top of the seat with Velcro, and I'd knocked it loose. Jose had already left—he said he had errands to run—but I went back into the house and found Lorraine. I brought her outside and showed her the tape recorder. "That Jose," she said, shaking her head. "It's one of those voice-activated things. He put that there to spy on you."

"Why?

"Because he's a psycho."

That may have been true, but I saw it differently: If Jose was that concerned about what I was up to, he must have really liked me. I left the tape recorder where it was, and I drove away smiling.

When I got to Orlando, I told Cathleen all about Jose, and even included this last bit about the tape recorder. "You shouldn't stay with him," she said. "He's cheating on you, and he thinks you're cheating on him."

"How do you know that?" I said, indignant.

"I had a boyfriend like that once. That's the way those guys are."

I guess that's one of those clichés that happen to be true. But I didn't buy it. I made the same mistake women have been making for thousands of years. I thought for sure I could change him. I thought Jose would change for me.

I spent two nights in Orlando and began to panic. I had to get back. If I didn't get back immediately, he'd find somebody else.

"I still think you're crazy," Cathleen said. "You deserve better."

"I know," I said. "That's a sweet thing to say."

"I just don't want you to get hurt."

I raced home, keeping my eyes peeled for the highway patrol, and made it back in record time without getting a speeding ticket. When I walked in, Jose wasn't around, but Ozzie's girlfriend, Lorraine, was out by the pool. I liked Lorraine. I went out and joined her.

"How was Orlando?" she asked.

"Good. Where's Jose?"

"I don't know," she said, with a bit of a lilt in her voice. "He and Ozzie are running around. Maybe at the gym."

Jose and Ozzie came back, and we went out to dinner. For a few days the four of us just hung out. I started feeling really comfortable around Lorraine, and when the boys were out, we'd sit by the pool and talk. She could see I was hopelessly in love with Jose, and I think she felt bad for me.

"Diane was here," she told me one morning, out by the pool. The boys were still asleep.

"Who?"

"Diane. One of his old girlfriends. She's friends with his sister too. She came by while you were away in Orlando."

I couldn't believe it. This was the same Diane who had been with him and his family in Texas, the one who left the very morning I arrived. "She spent the night?" I asked.

"No," Lorraine said. "She was just hanging around. Massaging his feet and stuff."

I felt physically ill. Lorraine asked me not to say anything, and I was careful. I went inside to confront Jose and found him on the phone. The first words I heard as I came up the stairs were clear and unmistakable: "I can't believe you're pregnant! You can't be pregnant!"

I opened the door and shouted, "What the fuck is going on here?!"

"Nothing," he said and hung up.

"Nothing? Who the fuck is pregnant? Was that Diane? Huh?

Was that your little friend Diane you were talking to? Did you get her pregnant?!"

"You're crazy!"

"Am I?"

There was this big sculpture on the dresser, a glass bird, and I grabbed it and smashed it on the floor.

"What the fuck are you doing? That was expensive!"

"Who were you talking to on the phone?!"

"Fuck you. Don't be shouting at me. That's what Esther used to do, and I'm not putting up with that shit."

"Maybe she did it for good reason! Were you cheating on her, too?!"

"Okay, that's it!" he shouted. "I'm getting this thing under control right now. I'm calling the police." He picked up the phone and dialed 911. "This is Jose Canseco, and I'm having a problem here." He got off the phone, more pissed than ever, and glares at me: "You're not going to do what Esther did. That's not happening."

"Esther, huh?! Why do you still have her fucking pictures all over the fucking house? Are you still in love with her, asshole?" I was shaking with rage. "Tell me if you fucked Diane, you bastard!"

I went over and pushed him, and he pushed me back, hard. I was in shock. "You son of a bitch!"

"You're crazy!" he said, storming toward the door. *"¡Estás completamente loca!"*

"How could you do this to me? Why am I even here? You were with Diane and she's pregnant!"

"She can't be pregnant! She's lying. She's a liar."

"How do you know she can't be pregnant?"

"I just know, okay?"

"But you fucked her?!"

"Fuck this!"

He left the room, and I collapsed on the bed, sobbing. A few minutes later, I heard the police coming up the drive. Jose let them in, and I could hear him telling them about me, and how I'd broken his precious glass bird and attacked him. He made it sound like I'd committed some major crime. I didn't understand what his point was. Was he going to have them charge me with destruction of property and assault? Did he want them to arrest me?

The police came up to the bedroom. "He's a liar and a cheater," I said, still crying. I must have looked like hell. They asked me if I was all right, and I pulled myself together and told them I was fine. But I wasn't fine. I was furious and felt betrayed and my heart was breaking.

"Why don't you sleep in separate rooms tonight?" one of the officers suggested. "I'm sure you'll both feel a lot better in the morning."

I took his advice. I went to a guest room and cried myself to sleep. Jose was cheating on me. I had known it all along, and now I had all the confirmation I needed—the confirmation I needed but didn't want. That's the honest truth. I didn't want to know Jose was cheating on me. I was crazy about him. I thought I was going to spend the rest of my life with him.

In the morning, Jose walked into the room and woke me up. I was still mad at him. "Why do you do this to me? How do you think I feel when I hear you on the phone with other women? Why do you still talk to your ex-wife all the time? Do you even care about my feelings?"

"Jessica, listen to me. I'm sorry about last night. I'm sorry about everything."

"Are you? Are you really?"

"Yes," he said, and it looked like tears were welling up in his eyes a little. "I really care about you. I love you." It was the first time he had said that, and he seemed as moved by it as I was. "This is hard for me, Jessica," he went on, and by this point he was crying. "Just, you know, me and Esther—it was hard when my marriage fell apart. And maybe I'm a little scared. But I'm crazy about you. I don't want to lose you."

It was the first time Jose had told me he loved me and the first time we seemed to be on the verge of having a real conversation. I wanted to keep it going, but I also wanted to clear up the ugly business that had brought us to this place. "What about Diane?"

"She's not pregnant."

"How do you know?"

"Because," he said, and he was having trouble with this, "because I'm on steroids."

"On what?"

"Steroids. It's this shit I take to make me more muscular. It makes me a better athlete."

"What does that have to do with Diane?"

"It affects your sperm count. I don't have viable sperm." He leaned down and kissed me. "I'm sorry. I need to know you forgive me."

"What is this steroid thing? Is it dangerous?"

"No, it's not dangerous. But I don't want to talk about it."

"Why not?"

"I just don't. Maybe some other time. Do you forgive me?" He kissed me again.

"Okay," I said. "I forgive you."

He had to go run some errands that morning, and I went out and sat by the pool with Lorraine. "How you doing?" she asked.

"Okay."

"I can't believe he called the cops."

"What do you know about steroids?" I asked.

"What do you want to know?"

"Everything."

"They shoot up. They mix up this different shit and shoot each other up in the butt."

"And he's doing that??"

"Half the players do it. You see how bulked up they get? You don't get that kind of muscle just working out. You need help."

"Jose too?"

"Him more than anyone."

"Seriously?"

"Didn't you notice his balls?"

"What about them?"

"How small they are? The steroids make them shrink up."

"So it's true his sperm's no good?"

"What have you been using for birth control?"

"Nothing," I said. "He told me he was taking care of it."

"There you go," she said. "He's on steroids. He knows he can't get you pregnant."

"I don't believe this."

"Don't you see how he has to pee all the time?" she said. "And look at that body on him. The guy eats at Burger King almost every day. Pure junk. And he's lazy as shit. He never works out, and he still looks like that. That's not an accident."

It was true. Jose could put away junk food like nobody's business, and he still looked great.

"When you're on steroids, you can eat whatever you want," Lorraine explained. "It turns all that shit into muscle."

"Now that you mention it," I said, "I think he's starting to look a little bloated."

"That's just the testosterone," Lorraine said. "He'll get it right."

It was all too much for me, so I switched the topic back to what I was really worried about: our endangered relationship. "I don't think things are going to work out for Jose and me," I said.

"Why do you say that?"

"Because he cheats all the time."

"That's just Jose," she said. "You're the one."

"What do you mean?"

"I mean, you're next," she said. "I was around when he met Esther, and he was exactly the same way. You could tell he wasn't going to let her go, and you can tell the same thing when he's around you. You'll see. He's always going to want you, even if he keeps cheating. All those other women, Diane, Sara, Miranda—they don't mean shit to him."

All this information was driving me crazy. When Jose came home, he walked out to the pool with a big smile and leaned down and gave me a big kiss. "How's my princess?" he asked.

"Okay."

"What are you two girls plotting?" he asked, still smiling. "You plotting something?"

"No," Lorraine said. "We're waiting for you and Ozzie. Where we going to dinner?"

"Wherever you want," he said and went back in the house.

"I'm going to go talk to him," I told Lorraine, and I went up to the bedroom.

Jose was getting undressed and about to hop in the shower. I wondered if he'd been with another woman and was about to wash her smell off his body, but I tried to not think about it.

"I want to know about the steroids," I said. "I'm worried about them."

"I told you. There's nothing to worry about. I just take a little tiny bit from time to time."

"Why are you so bloated? Are you taking testosterone?"

"What are you talking about?"

Then I started thinking about the other women in his life, and I couldn't help myself. I knew I shouldn't say anything, and I fought it, but the words just tumbled out of me. "Who's Sara?" I asked. "Who's Miranda?"

He turned to look at me, pissed, and stormed out in his underwear without saying anything. I felt bad. I hadn't meant to narc on Lorraine, but the desire to know the truth was stronger than the need to protect her. I followed him outside and found him by the pool, waving his arms and shouting at her. "What the fuck is wrong with you, *mujer?* You got a big mouth on you!"

"Jose!" I said. "Leave her alone. Why are you getting mad at her? You told me about the steroids yourself!"

He turned around and stormed past me into the house, not saying anything, and I looked over at Lorraine, feeling like crap. "I'm sorry," I said.

I heard Jose's voice booming from inside the house. "Ozzie! Tell your goddamn girlfriend to keep her big mouth shut, understand?! I'm not fucking around here!"

I looked back at Lorraine again. She seemed more resigned than angry. I guess she was used to the Canseco brothers. She gave me a little shrug. "Jose is jealous of us," she explained. "He thinks we're getting too friendly."

"What? I'm not allowed to have friends?"

I went back in the house and rejoined Jose in the bedroom. I went over and kissed him and acted all sweet. Jose was like putty when I was sweet. "It wasn't Lorraine's fault," I said, kissing his neck. "Please don't take it out on her."

"She's full of shit," he said.

"I just want to know, for me," I said. "About the steroids. About these other girls. I won't get mad," I went on, practically cooing. "Like who's this Sara girl? Did you sleep with her?"

"It didn't mean anything," he said. "She's this little groupie. I fucked her, and it was nothing. She's nothing."

"You fucked her?!" I shrieked, no longer cooing. "You son of a bitch! Why do you have to fuck everything that moves?!"

"Hey!" he snapped, whirling to face me. "You *asked!* You

don't want to know, don't fucking ask! But don't fucking get mad at me for telling you the truth!"

He had a point. I didn't say anything. He went off to take a shower. By the time he got back, I was somewhat calm. "Will you tell me about the steroids at least?"

"What do you want to know?"

"Everything."

He went into the closet and pulled out a big duffel bag and set it on the bed. There was a ton of stuff in there: vials of Winstrol, Anadrol, Deca-Durabolin, and a bunch of other junk with names I couldn't even pronounce. Pills, too. And literally hundreds of syringes.

"How do you do it?" I asked.

"In the butt mostly," he said.

"You inject yourself?"

"Yeah. Usually. Or I get my brother or one of the other players to help me. You want to do me?"

"No way. I'm afraid of needles."

Jose laughed. He said there was nothing to it and started showing me how it was done, getting the solution ready and filling the syringe. It gave me the creeps. I could hardly look at it. He turned around and pointed at a spot high on his butt. "This is where you need to put it."

"Me? I'm not doing it. What if I hit a nerve?"

"Don't be silly. It's a piece of cake. Go on. Just stick it in."

He put the syringe in my hand and leaned over. For a few moments, I couldn't do it. "What are you waiting for?" he asked.

"Okay," I said, shutting my eyes and bracing myself. "Here it goes."

I jabbed him, expecting him to yelp, but he didn't yelp. I opened my eyes, and he seemed fine. I looked at the empty syringe.

"See?" he said. "Nothing to it."

And that was the beginning of my involvement with the steroid thing. Pretty soon, it was routine. Jose would mix up a batch, acting like he was a chemist or something, then he'd lean over and take his punishment like a man. I began to enjoy it.

The strangest thing about it was that it brought us closer together. I guess there was a level of intimacy to jabbing my boyfriend in the ass with a big needle, and for a while things calmed down between us.

When the mysterious Diane called to admit that she wasn't pregnant, Jose got off the phone and told me he would never sleep with another woman again. "I'm turning over a new leaf," he said. "I don't want any other woman. I only want you."

He also began to make a habit of telling me how much he loved me. After the first time, I guess it came easy. I started to believe what Lorraine had told me that day by the pool: that I was the one and he would never let me go.

One night, I went into the bathroom and cried, but I was crying from happiness. I was desperately in love with Jose, and Jose was desperately in love with me.

Or so he told me.

Plastic Surgery

For several months during that off-season, we settled into a pleasant routine, and—with the exception of the constant phone calls from Esther and the occasional call from yet another mystery bimbo—life was fun.

I started going to the gym with Jose, pushing him to stop being so lazy, and I tried to keep him away from junk food. As a result, I found myself getting into the best shape of my life.

I was worried about him and about the long-term effects of steroids on his body, which I knew couldn't be as negligible as he suggested. So I started reading everything I could on the subject. I read a lot of articles in fitness magazines, and my mother began to send me medical journals. Before long I was something of an expert on steroids. Curiously enough, I found that I was able to retain most of what I read. This was a far cry from my experience in school, and I guess the difference was obvious: I was genuinely interested in the subject.

I learned that steroids were related to the male sex hormones but were man-made and used for medical purposes, especially with patients whose illnesses were causing them to waste away. Steroids had become the drug of choice for many athletes, who were interested in enhancing both their performance and appearance. This was not only illegal but also dangerous. Some of the more serious side effects were said to include liver and kidney tumors and cancer.

"The stuff's going to kill you," I told Jose.

"No it's not," he said. "Those people don't know what they're talking about."

There were plenty of other articles in my fitness magazines, and I read them, too. Before long I started thinking about becoming a personal trainer. I kept working out and pushing Jose to work out, and both of us were beginning to look very good. One of the trainers at the gym saw the transformation in me, and he told me about the Fitness America Pageant, which was holding regionals in October in Dallas. He said he thought I should compete. I told Jose about it, and he was very supportive, and when October rolled around, we flew to Dallas together.

I ended up winning, and I was slated to go to the finals the following month in Redondo Beach, California. I was ecstatic and feeling absolutely terrific about myself, and Jose seemed just as pleased. Then I was approached to do a magazine cover with Michael O'Hearn, the power-lifting champion, and my self-esteem got another huge boost.

Unfortunately, that turned into a disaster. Jose came to the shoot and stood there, lurking on the sidelines, arms crossed, pacing and fuming. He didn't like the way we were being posed—he thought it looked cheesy and cheap—and he made a stink with the magazine people, totally belittling me in front of them. "I'm not going to be with a girl who wants to do shit like this," he said. I was totally humiliated. In the end, the magazine decided to not run the pictures, and Jose and I went home. He was angry for days, and I did my best to appease him. I found myself apologizing and telling him it would never happen again, even though I still wasn't sure what, exactly, had happened, or even why I was apologizing.

Jose began to take off again, and I suspected he was beginning to see other girls. He and Ozzie would go out on the boat, leaving me and Lorraine by the pool. And when they got back, he never had anything to say.

Sometimes, uncharacteristically, the guys would actually ask me and Lorraine if we wanted to ride on the boat with them, but you could see they didn't mean it. I'd look in Jose's eyes and see that he was hoping I'd say no. So I always said no, and Lorraine always said no. But we'd always be real sweet about it.

"No, but thank you for asking."

"You sure?"

"That's okay, honey. You boys go on ahead. Have a good time."

As soon and he and Ozzie were out of earshot, I'd always say the same thing: "I don't want to go on your fucking boat!"

Lorraine would laugh, and we'd smoke a little grass together and just veg out by the pool. "I know they're cruising for girls," she said. "The only thing those guys ever think about is getting laid."

"I wish I knew for sure," I said.

"I'm sure," Lorraine said. "And you should be sure, too. When Jose showers before going to the pet store, he's not going to the pet store."

She was right, but I had a gift for self-delusion. Jose only showered every second or third day, and always before going off on some imaginary errand. I didn't want to face this because the facts didn't correspond to all the wonderful things I wanted to believe about him and about our magical future together.

Then I started getting bacterial infections. Jose sent me to see a doctor who was probably in cahoots with him. "I'm not sure what you've got," the doctor told me. "It's not serious. I think it's just vaginal bacteria. You can get these from towels."

"What towels?" I'd ask. "I only use the towels at the house."

"Well, it's hard to tell with these things. Sometimes they just come and go, like a cold."

This was no common cold. Jose was bringing something home to me, and it was on his dick.

He didn't want to talk about it, though. If I said anything, he'd take me shopping, or he'd hand me a few hundred dollars and tell me to go shopping on my own. Or he'd tell me to get my nails done or that I could use a facial. He kept trying to improve me, to make me perfect, and I wasn't sure I'd ever be improved enough. I'd seen pictures of Esther around the house and that was a lot to compete with.

There was a pattern there: He'd either deflect or attack. Attacking seemed much more effective. It spoke to my lack of self-esteem. A little comment about my hair could plunge me into a deep depression.

One day, after I'd gone back to the doctor for a third time—to deal with yet another unidentifiable infection—I was questioning Jose about his dalliances with a little more vigor than usual, and I found him staring at my nose.

"What?" I asked.

"Nothing," he said, but he kept staring at my nose.

"That's not true. You're staring at my nose."

"Am I?"

He continued to stare, so I came right out and asked him. "If there was one thing you could fix about me, any little thing, what would it be?"

"I don't know," he said. "I think your nose is cute, but if it bothers you and you want to do something about it, talk to Lorraine. She's thinking of doing hers."

I was crushed. He hated my nose. Maybe that was the problem. If I had my nose fixed, maybe he'd stop seeing other girls.

I talked to Lorraine, who'd already done some research on local plastic surgeons, and we ended up having our noses done at the same time. I told the doctor that I just wanted mine thinned out a little, nothing too radical, and he showed me a book full of photographs of noses. It was very confusing. It was like being at a restaurant or something and picking a nose out of a menu.

I found one I liked, sort of, and went in for surgery, then I went home to recuperate. For several days, with my face all swollen and bandaged up, I refused to leave the bedroom. I sat there crying and only stopped crying when Vera came in with something to eat. She felt very bad for me. Jose was hardly around. But for once I didn't mind his absence: With the bandages and the puffy eyes and everything, I felt like a freak, and I didn't want him to see me like that. Still, I wondered why I had let him talk me into a nose job. Where had my self-respect gone, and had I had any to begin with?

When the bandages finally came off, I started sobbing all over again. I didn't like my nose. The doctor said it was still raw and swollen and that the swelling would go down in time—it would look perfectly fine soon. He was right, sort of, but I still didn't like it. Jose, however, seemed to think it was pretty cute, so I decided that the surgery had been a good idea after all. How pathetic is that? It was never about *my* feelings; it was all about Jose. Even my thoughts no longer counted.

After my plastic surgery, we settled back into our routine. We'd go the gym, lounge by the pool, play with the animals, go to bed, fuck, watch movies, and pass out. I was still thinking about becoming a personal trainer, and I'd contacted the Aerobics and Fitness Association of America (AFAA) about becoming certified. They sent me a bunch of material, and I began studying for the test. It was challenging and stimulating. I certainly wasn't getting much mental stimulation from Jose, who pretty much liked to sleep, fuck, and eat, though not necessarily in that order. And the animals were fun, but they had about as much to say to me as Jose.

However, I was getting more used to Jose's sexual style, though I can't honestly say I was enjoying it. Then again, it wasn't about me. Jose's favorite position was any position where he could watch himself in the mirrors. If he could have made love to a clone of himself, I'm sure that would have been the ultimate high.

I should have said something, but I didn't, so in some ways I only had myself to blame. I remember thinking that I was turning into my mother. She had spent her whole life with a man who gave absolutely no thought to her wants and needs, and only much later had she gone into nursing, finally doing something for herself. I wondered if Jose was some sort of father figure, but I didn't wonder very much: I didn't want to know that much about myself. I found it kind of frightening.

Early that December, Jose and his brother got into a big fight, and he kicked him and Lorraine out of the house. I think part of it was connected to my relationship with her—Jose thought she was a bad influence and that she revealed too much about his horrible past and his behavior with women—but the rest of it was purely connected to Jose's mounting frustrations. Months earlier he had told me he was sick of baseball, but it looked to me like he needed baseball to keep himself going.

We never talked about it, though. We never talked about anything.

That Christmas, he flew my parents down to Miami, and they stayed in the house with us for a few days. Everyone was very cordial. Jose showed my father his car collection, and on a couple of occasions he took us out on the boat. They liked hanging out by the pool, and they loved the animals, especially the big iguana and the two cats. It was all very pleasant, and Jose was on his best, most charming behavior.

Still, with Lorraine gone, I only had my mother to talk to, and I told her about some of the things that were going on. I said I thought Jose was still cheating on me, and I mentioned the constant calls from his ex-wife. I also admitted that I enjoyed the lifestyle. It beat working at Hooters, and it was way more fun than college. She was understanding; *too* understanding. She should have slapped me across the face, told me to pull myself together, and urged me to get a life of my own. But that wasn't my mother. And really, when I think about it, it wasn't her responsibility.

When I told her that Jose was doing steroids, she wasn't happy about it. My mom was a nurse, and she knew even more about steroids than I did. She said they were unhealthy on every level—physical, mental, and emotional—and she questioned me about his moods. I had not known Jose in his pre-steroid days, but he was definitely a moody guy. I didn't think he was exceptionally moody, though, especially when I tried to put it in the context of his entire history. That lousy childhood, with a father who never tired of belittling him; his mother's death when he was nineteen; the effects of early success; the ugly divorce. . . . If I thought about it, it seemed to me that he was entitled to a little moodiness.

"I still don't like it," my mother said. "Nobody really knows that much about the long-term effects, but they're definitely not good."

Eventually, we dropped the subject and concentrated on having a good time. Jose bought me a beautiful Omega watch for Christmas with diamonds all around the face, and I bought him some clothes, a new wallet, and a few other things, all of which I billed to the credit card he'd given me, and which he dutifully paid when the bill arrived.

Ozzie came by to visit with his new girlfriend, Amy. I felt

kind of bad for Lorraine, but Amy was real sweet and funny, and I liked her right away.

When my parents were ready to return to Cleveland, Jose and I took them to the airport. And on the way back to the house, Jose said something very touching. "I like the way you interact with your family. I like the way you respect each other. I can't stand families where all they ever do is scream at each other."

Now, looking back on that day, I don't know why I found it so touching. Now it strikes me as a good thing if a family gets emotional enough to scream at one another. It wasn't so much that my parents and I respected one another, but rather that we remained oddly disconnected. Jose didn't have a clue about my childhood, just as I only had the vaguest inkling about his. If I knew then what I know now, I may have had a better idea of what was going on. Jose was abusing me, as he himself had been abused and belittled. And I was taking it, as I'd learned to take it by watching my mother.

"I like the fact that you're not like Esther on any level," Jose went on. "She was flashy and liked attention, and she was always looking for trouble. I couldn't trust her."

Implicit in that remark was the notion that he could trust me, but somehow it didn't work out that way. I found out a short while later that Jose was having me followed by a private investigator, so clearly there wasn't much room for logic in Jose's steroid-addled brain. It was only then that I remembered the tape recorder that he'd left in the Suburban, which had happened just months before. It struck me that he had his own insecurity issues. Why else would he think I was cheating on him?

"I want to see the videotape," I overheard Jose saying on the phone one day, and I became suddenly attentive. I inched closer to the open bedroom door. "I don't care, Javier," he said. "*No me importa.* I want the tape."

He got the tape the next day, and I waited until he had locked himself in the bedroom before going up to confront him.

"Jose, open the door. What are you doing in there?"

"Nothing. Go away."

He finally relented. I went in and knew he'd been watching the videotape, so I crossed directly to the VCR and turned it on. It was footage of Amy and me at the local park on the swings. I was twenty-one years old, and I was swinging my life away. Isn't that sad?

"So who's Javier?" I said, turning to face Jose. "You have a private investigator following me?"

"Not really," he said, looking sheepish.

"You're wasting your money, Jose. I'm not cheating on you. I'm not like you."

"Leave me alone."

"No. You leave me alone. You're the only one who cheats around here. Is that why you don't trust me? Because you think I'm a cheater like you?"

"I don't trust Amy."

"Really? She and your brother are going to get married. What is it you don't trust about her? And why is trusting her any of your business? And what does it have to do with me, come to think of it?"

"You ask too many questions," he said.

"I'm not cheating on you, Jose. I'm right here at home with the cats and the iguana and the turtle. There's no one else, and I don't want anyone else."

He walked out of the room, and I decided not to follow him out. I didn't need to get into a big argument. I'd said my part. Also, in a strange way, I found the whole thing kind of flattering. The fact that Jose cared enough to have me followed around counted for something, right? In *my* addled brain, which at that point was free of drugs, it showed he cared.

But if he cared, why was his ex-wife still calling two to three times a week? Why were her pictures all over the house? Why wouldn't he let me redecorate the damn place or find a new one altogether? Why was his little pager buzzing all the time? And why was he taking showers *before* going to the gym?

I called Cathleen in Orlando to vent a little. I was paying half the rent on the apartment, with Jose's money, admittedly, but every time I talked about going to visit her he told me not to go. He didn't ask me. He *told* me.

"What?" Cathleen said. "You're his prisoner? Why are you letting him control you?"

"I'm not," I said. "He just wants me here."

"You should leave him. He's no good for you."

"It's just that macho thing. It's cultural. He thinks he has to keep an eye on me."

"I'm not even talking about that. That's the least of it. I'm talking about the way he cheats on you all the time. It's not going to end."

I was so confused. I loved Jose. If I had learned anything

from Cathleen that day, it was that I had three choices: I could take it like my mother had done her whole life. I could figure out how to make things right. Or I could leave. Any way I looked at it, it was up to me. Any way I looked at it, it was my fault.

Leaving him was not an option, though. Leaving Jose would have been an admission of defeat.

Now, these many years later, I see that *staying* was the real defeat.

7

CHAPTER

The Enabler

Early in 1994, I decided my nose didn't look right and went back to have more work done on it. It had nothing to do with my nose, of course. My nose was fine. It was just another manifestation of my illness. Having my nose done was like going shopping. It gave my mind a chance to focus on something other than what I needed to be focusing on. It was an escape.

After surgery, I went home to recuperate and thought obsessively about my nose. When the bandages came off, I couldn't tell whether I liked it, but I could certainly tell that I was having a little trouble breathing. The doctor told me not to worry. It was scar tissue, and my nose was still inflamed. It would get better. It didn't.

One night, we were having sex, and Jose was taking me from behind, and I looked up and saw my nose in the mirror. I thought I looked awful, and I burst into tears.

"What's wrong?" Jose asked.

I rolled off to one side. "Nothing," I said, still sobbing. "It's me."

"What is?"

"Don't worry about it. I'm just a little upset. It's got nothing to do with you."

"Okay," he said. He got out of bed, slipped into his shorts, and left the room. I couldn't believe he was that uninterested in what was troubling me. He could have tried to comfort me, or pushed a little to get to the bottom of things, but he simply didn't care.

When he came back, I had the crying under control, but I was still shaky and upset. He sat down on the bed and turned on the TV without so much as looking at me. "If you want to talk about it, talk about it," he said. "But I'm not going to beg you to talk about it."

He made it seem like it was my fault. And maybe it was. Maybe I should have been more frank about everything. My unhappiness. The infidelity. The complete and total lack of intimacy. The lousy sex.

"I just feel bad about my nose," I said.

"There's nothing wrong with your nose," he said. "It's a lot better than your old nose."

Jose must have thought that was a nice thing to say. He was reaching out to me across the vast chasm that defined our relationship, and now he was done reaching, and he was looking for something good on TV. There was nothing good on TV, but anything was better than talking to me.

I went downstairs and called home. My mother answered, and I told her about my second nose job. "I don't understand why you had the first one," she said. "I always thought you had a lovely nose."

"I never liked it," I said. "Even in high school, I thought it was too big for my face. When Jose pointed it out, he was only telling me what I already knew."

The next day I was out by the pool, flipping through a magazine, when I saw a picture of a monitor lizard. I told Jose I thought it would be cool to have one. He came home that afternoon with a three-foot monitor lizard. I was thrilled. Jose had a hard time communicating, but the lizard said it all.

I felt like Sally Field at the Academy Awards: "You like me! You really like me!" I was only about twelve when I'd seen that on TV, but it stayed with me. I think it stayed with a lot of people. At the end of the day, we all want to be loved. Most of us just aren't that public about it.

After I spoke to my mother, I called Lorraine, who had moved to an apartment in Miami. "I don't know what to do about Jose," I said. "I keep telling myself I love him, but is love really supposed to feel like this?"

"Don't ask me, girl. I have no idea."

"Sometimes I think I only stay for the perks," I said, floored by my own honesty.

"Well," she said, "the perks *are* pretty good."

I don't know what I thought. Did I think my life would fall apart if I didn't have the big house and the fast cars and the nice clothes? Probably. Was it wrong to think like that? I'd heard the old cliché: *I've been rich, and I've been poor, and—trust me—rich is better.* And it *was* better. But how much better? If I had stayed with Steve, I probably wouldn't be driving around in a Lamborghini, but would I have been less unhappy?

Maybe. I didn't know. It seemed life was full of maybes. Everything was unknowable.

In February, Jose went to Arizona for spring training, and he wanted me to go with him, but I told him I needed a few days to get ready. The truth is, I was actually giving some thought to my future. I was tired of our life, tired of making excuses for him, tired of searching for yet another reason to stick around. This wasn't a relationship. On an emotional level, Jose and I couldn't have been less connected. But physically, the pull was too strong. His mere presence was enough to reduce me to jelly, and I simply couldn't think when he was around. I needed a little distance to clear my head and figure out the future.

The truth is, I *wanted* to leave him. The perks were nice, sure, but they weren't enough. And I thought if I could find one more reason to leave—just one convincing little sign—I'd be able to pack my bags and take the hell off.

The day after he left for Arizona, I picked up the phone and dialed in for his messages. The operator asked me for the code, and I gave it to her, and the very first message knocked the wind out of me: "I'm twenty minutes away. Be there soon. I love you."

I flipped. I called him in Arizona and confronted him, and he said he didn't know what I was talking about.

"Call your answering service!" I screamed. "They'll give you your goddamn message."

"I don't know what you're talking about. That's an old page. I told that girl not to come that time. I hate her."

"Just another slab of 'road beef,' eh?"

"Jessica—"

"When are you going to stop lying to me?!"

"Listen—"

"Fuck you! I'm done listening to you. I'm leaving. I'm getting my stuff and moving out."

I slammed down the receiver and stormed off to pack, but I ended up collapsing on the bed. He called and called, and I refused to pick up the phone. Finally, Vera answered. She came to the door of the bedroom and asked me to please take the call. "Mr. Canseco is very upset," she said.

I reached for the receiver. "What are you going to lie about now?" I snapped.

"Nothing," he said. "I'm not going to lie anymore. I'm not going to cheat anymore. I love you. Please forgive me. Please come to Arizona."

I was crying so hard I couldn't answer, and I hung up and drew myself a bath. I called Amy, Ozzie's girlfriend, to see if she could help. But she couldn't help. "What are you going to do with your life if you leave?" she asked me.

It was a good question. I had been asking myself that very question for a long time. I didn't have a clue. "I guess I could move to Orlando with Cathleen," I said. "Or I could stay in Miami and move in with Lorraine."

"I don't know what to tell you," Amy said.

I drove to South Beach to see Lorraine. She thought I should leave him and move in with her, but those things are never as easy as they seem. At that level of addiction, I wasn't responding to logic, I was responding to emotion—and my heart kept telling me, right or wrong, that I was in love with Jose.

The next day I flew to Arizona. Jose was very happy to see me. When baseball season started, we went back to Colleyville, and Jose had the entire menagerie shipped to the house.

In the days ahead, peace reigned and the pager didn't go off and I felt marginally more secure. After all, Jose had begged me not to leave him, right? And he was behaving himself. I felt prettier, too, and I even began to like my nose. I was also dressing better—the gold shorts and the collared shirts were ancient history—and I felt like more of an adult. *This is finally working,* I told myself.

We began hanging around with some of the other players and that was nice, too. I felt like the serious girlfriend now, not like a marginalized groupie. Jose was showing me off. He was making a statement.

This was also the year that the steroid thing began to get out of hand. Jose and I were out to dinner one night with another ball player and his wife, and the guy began to ask Jose about steroids. Jose was a big proponent of steroids. To hear him talk, the future of professional sports depended on steroids. Why shouldn't an athlete be the best athlete he could be? It sounded like a bizarre version of that old TV series, *The Six Million Dollar Man.* Bigger. Stronger. Faster. Better.

We took the other couple back to the house and into our bedroom, and Jose pulled out the duffel bag. Even the player's wife was into it. She said she felt a little heavy and was interested in losing weight, and Jose told her that steroids made you practically immune to junk food.

It turned into a steroid party. Jose mixed up a batch for each of them, explaining what he was doing and acting like some kind of pharmacist. He shot the guy up before he sent him on his way, and when we went to bed that night, he seemed to be feeling pretty good about the whole thing. "You just watch," he said. "You're going to see this guy's game improve like you won't believe."

He was right. Within four weeks, the guy was hitting them out of the park, but he looked bloated. Jose took him aside and told him to cut back on the testosterone, and he lost the bloat almost immediately. In the weeks and months ahead, a lot of players were talking about steroids and going to Jose for advice.

As far as I know, Jose wasn't selling them. He wasn't interested in that. I think they were readily available on the Internet and through direct mail from a few pharmaceutical companies. I really don't know the details. All I know is that nobody made a big fuss. They talked about them openly. They were no more secretive than a pair of housewives discussing a favorite recipe, and they all had their favorite recipes. They didn't even bother hiding the stuff in their luggage. Jose would stick a bunch of syringes in a shoe, to keep them from breaking, and he'd wrap the various canisters in T-shirts. Nobody thought there was anything wrong with any of it, and none of them had any idea it was going to turn into such a huge scandal.

I'd like to say I was just the naive little girlfriend playing along, but I was more of an enabler. I knew too much about them to condone their use, but I did nothing. On the contrary, I knew so much about them that I was turning into Jose's lab assistant, intent on helping him develop the perfect winning formula.

If he was a little bloated, I'd make him cut down on the

testosterone and give him an extra dose of Winstrol. When he started getting injured, I amped up the decas. And when he lost interest in sex, we re-upped the testosterone.

I no longer had any trouble with needles. He'd bend over, I'd give him a playful slap on the rump, and boom—we were done. All that was missing was a little nurse's cap.

The one thing that seemed more pronounced to me were the mood swings, but I couldn't be sure about those. I think I had read so much about them that I began to look for them, and maybe I noticed things that weren't really there. As I said earlier, I didn't know Jose pre-steroids, so I had no old Jose to compare him with.

The funny thing is that neither of us really knew what we were doing. Jose pretended that he approached these drugs as if he were a scientist, but, as far as I could see, he was the least scientific scientist in the world. It was basically a guessing game. If he was hitting a lot of runs one week, he would check the log to see what we were pumping into him just then. If it was some combination of Winstrol and testosterone, for example, he thought that to be the magic home run formula.

If his joints hurt, he'd adjust accordingly, blaming whatever he was on *that* week. And if he found himself getting injured a lot, he'd adjust the formula to see how it might change things.

He read about steroids in bodybuilding magazines, just as I had, and he talked to guys at the gym, but there was no science involved and no doctors. Jose thought he had the answers. And so did everyone else. Jose looked good, and everyone wanted to look as good as he did. The players were going through the shit like candy.

Strangely enough, with the exception of that one time, when Jose and I brought that player and his wife back to our house and walked them through the routine, the women never talked about steroids. When I asked Jose about it, he got angry. "That's the way it is," he said. "The women don't talk about it. *¿Comprende?* Whenever the women talk, bad things happen."

"So what's the message here?" I said, an edge creeping into my voice. "We keep our mouths shut?"

"Yeah," he said. "That's exactly right. Steroids, none of their business. You see something on the road, none of their business. You don't tell anyone. Only me. If you talk, it's going to get back to me one way or another, and it's not going to be good. For you. For me. Or for the team."

The following night, one of the wives left, and later that same evening I saw her husband walking into his room with a little bimbo. I told Jose, and he got mad again. "It's none of our business. Didn't I tell you already?" He *had* told me, but I still felt bad about it.

The next day I was at lunch with two other wives, and I had to fight the urge to discuss what I'd seen. I did ask them about this odd code of silence, however. It felt like that omerta thing with the mob, or whatever it is they call it, where you pay with your life if you betray your friends.

"That's just the way it is," one of the women said. "You don't talk about those things. It causes problems."

"But if I saw your husband with another woman, wouldn't you want me to tell you?"

"Frankly, no," she said, then turned her attention to lunch.

"*I'd* like to know."

"Why?" she asked. "You already know, and you're living with it. Why would you want someone to rub your face in it? It'll just hurt you, and it'll create problems for everyone."

I was getting the picture. If she told me something about Jose, I'd confront Jose, and Jose would then confront this woman's husband. It was a bad business all around, and I guess everyone felt better about having rules. It reminded me of the day I had inadvertently ratted out Lorraine. That hadn't been much fun at all, for her or for me.

Ironically, when I got back to the hotel that day, I ran into the wife of Ivan Rodriguez, Maribel. She liked me, and she knew Jose, and I guess she didn't want me to get hurt. "I shouldn't be telling you this, and if Ivan finds out, he's going to get very pissed. But I think you should ask Jose what his ex-wife was doing with him in Detroit."

"What?" I asked, taken aback.

"It didn't come from me, okay?"

When Jose showed up in the room, I'd been stewing for hours. "So," I said, arms crossed in front of me. "You want to tell me about you and Esther in Detroit?"

"What are you talking about?"

"I know, Jose. Don't deny it, okay? I can't take anymore bullshit."

"Who told you?"

"No one you know," I said. "Just tell me."

"Nothing happened," he said. "I didn't tell Esther to come."

"Jesus Christ, Jose," I said and began to cry. "When is this going to end?"

"I'm telling you! Nothing happened. She came up for a day and told me she was lonely, and I sent her home."

"Are you sure?"

"Jessica, that relationship is over. I'm with you. I don't want anybody else."

I desperately wanted to believe him, so I believed him. He hugged me, and I calmed down a little, and now it was his turn to be upset. "So who told you, anyway?" he asked again.

"I don't know," I lied. "Someone called the room. I didn't recognize her voice."

"Those fucking wives," he grumbled. "They better learn how to keep their mouths shut."

Most of them did keep their mouths shut. That had been the exception. I was at lunch a few days later, with three of them, and they all looked absolutely radiant. "Do you ever worry about your husbands cheating on you?" I asked.

"My husband doesn't cheat," one of them said, and the others seemed to concur. I couldn't believe it. Jose had told me that the husband of one of these wives sitting with me was seriously into strippers, and he'd warned me not to share that information with *anyone.*

"Mine doesn't cheat either," another wife said. "If he did, I'd cut off his balls."

"If you can find them," the first one said.

We all laughed—this was a not-so-subtle reference to the effects of steroids—but after I stopped laughing, I didn't feel so great. These women all seemed kind of damaged and delusional, just like me. They wanted to talk about safe topics: clothes, shoes, meals, diets, and Pilates. Anything that may shatter the happy marriage myth was off limits, and we were all living our own versions of the myth.

These women would never venture beyond the surface. We would greet one another with air kisses, and we'd run down to Bloomingdale's together, but we wouldn't talk about anything that mattered. Life was so much easier when you refused to think.

Jose certainly didn't think. He was clueless. He would come home with girls' names and phone numbers scrawled on pieces of papers, stashed in various pockets. He would leave his cell phone by the side of the bed, and I'd scroll through the log and find one call after another: Kate, Cynthia, Deborah, Ashley.

One night, he came back to the hotel with a big stuffed teddy bear, and he said some girl had left it for him at the front desk. "What do you want?" he snapped. "I have fans."

He had a point. It wasn't his fault that women threw themselves at him. If he bent them over the bed, that was different. That *was* his fault. But that big teddy bear didn't mean anything. Right?

When I got mad, he'd yell that I was a nag, or, worse, that I was crazy. I remember showing him his phone log one time, as if that somehow confirmed my worst suspicions, and he had an answer for that, too. "I lent my phone to another player. His battery went dead. I don't know anyone called Jeannie, and I don't know anyone called Lucy."

It was possible.

Another time, I saw him writing a check to Esther—I guess it was an alimony payment—and it just killed me. Then I realized he had no control over that and that I had no right to get upset with him. I couldn't very well be jealous of his past, could I? Or I could, but what was the point? What would that have done for either of us?

So I started trying to think more like an adult. I turned my attention to the future. I thought we might get married and that would change everything. Ozzie and Amy were talking about getting married, and they seemed happy. I thought we could be happy, too, just like married couples everywhere.

I stopped nagging him, and I guess it made him wonder what had changed, and whether I was up to something. One time I was out at a movie with Jackie, the girlfriend of his teammate Juan Gonzalez, and some guy followed us inside. He must have been the worst private investigator in the world. He followed us back to the car, and when I told him to stop following us, he got flustered and hurried away.

I got back to the room and asked Jose why he was wasting his money. "I stopped nagging you, and what? You think I'm out cheating on you? Is that it? Would you like it better if I went back to nagging? Would that make you happy?"

"I don't want to talk about it," he said.

"I'm not like you, Jose. When I'm with a man, I'm really with him. I don't believe in cheating."

Amy and Ozzie came to visit. They looked very happy. One day Jose went on a road trip, and Ozzie went with him. The next day, feeling bored, I called a friend in Miami and asked her to send me some Ecstasy. A Federal Express envelope arrived the following morning. There was a copy of *The Three Little Pigs* in it, with a note clipped to the front: "Turn to page 24." There were six tabs of Ecstasy taped to the page.

I offered some to Amy, but she chickened out. I took one tab that very afternoon and before long I was rolling. When it began to take effect, I felt as good as I had ever felt in my life. I was laughing, glad to be alive, and the whole world seemed like a happy, wonderful place. Drugs will do that to you. Rolling was *it.*

After I came down, I told Amy, "I didn't know anything like that existed. It's so good it's dangerous."

"That's what I heard," she said.

I knew the drug was not without its risks—panic attacks, memory loss, liver failure, and even death. I wasn't going to make a habit of this—I was still into my fitness craze and still hoping to pursue the trainer thing—but for a few hours the drug did its job; for a few hours I didn't even *think* about Jose.

CHAPTER 8

The Big O

Shortly after a strike was called, Jose and I returned to Miami. It had been a pretty good season for him, but he kept getting injured. His hip was bothering him, the surgery on his arm hadn't quite worked out as planned, and now even his back was beginning to give him trouble. The fact is that Jose didn't have a large enough frame to carry all of that steroid-enhanced muscle. It was as if his body were beginning to shut down. It couldn't take the abuse.

I think he sensed it, too. When we got home, as if to make up for it, he said he wanted to move into a new house. He found a 20,000-square-foot Mediterranean-style mansion in Weston, Florida, about forty-five minutes north of Miami. It was huge, with a guesthouse, gym, and massive pool, all spread over four nicely manicured acres.

"Why do we need all this space?" I asked him. "We're not even married."

"I like it. I'm tired of Miami."

I thought he was overdoing it, trying to salve his bruised ego, but I didn't want to argue with him, so I tried to look on the bright side. We were breaking with the past, putting some distance between ourselves and the ghost of his ex-wife. I let myself become hopeful again. I thought Jose and I would finally settle down.

For the next few months, we were preoccupied with the move. It was a major ordeal, but we slowly got it together. The house seemed even larger than I originally thought. Vera was overwhelmed. "How am I going to manage this place? It's too big for just one person." Jose didn't care. He didn't want a staff. He trusted her. He told her to do the best she could.

Right after we settled in, Ozzie and Amy came to visit. The boys would work out in the gym or go golfing, and Amy and I would lounge by the pool.

By this time, Amy was pregnant, and I was happy for her but also a little jealous. Her life seemed to be moving forward, while mine was still in neutral.

The day after they left, I was sitting by the pool, leafing through a magazine, wondering what kind of mother I'd make, when I came across an ad for a cougar. It was hard to believe. A man in Plantation, Florida, was selling cougars. There was another guy selling lynx, and still another ad for bobcats. A big cat wasn't a child exactly, but it sounded kind of cool.

"We have so much property," I told Jose. "Wouldn't it be great to have a cougar?"

"Sure," he said. "I'd love a cougar. Why don't you make some calls?"

Now that we were all moved in, he was a little absent again. When he wasn't playing golf, he was worrying about the coming season. He suspected he was going to be traded, and he hated living with that kind of uncertainty.

Sometimes he'd come home after golf smelling of something other than golf. I wondered if he was cheating on me again, but I was afraid to say anything. I didn't want to rock the boat. I wanted to move to the next level. I wanted to have what Amy and Ozzie had.

Whenever I felt blue, I would lock myself up in my huge walk-in closet, surrounded by my things. I had begun to collect books by this time, still hungering for a little intellectual stimulation, and they were piled everywhere. I liked anything health-related, and I liked books about psychology. I was trying to educate myself, trying to make up for everything I'd missed in college.

Everything I owned in the world was in that closet, and just being there made me feel safe. It was my own private sanctuary. Sometimes Jose would come home and find me there. "What are you doing in the closet?" he'd ask.

"Nothing," I'd say. "Reading. Thinking."

If he wanted to know what I was thinking about, he didn't ask.

In December 1994, we found out that he'd been traded to Boston. He wasn't exactly thrilled, but I liked the idea because my sister Samantha lived there. I thought I would feel less isolated in Boston. I didn't have many close friends in Miami. There was Amy, who was busy making a life for herself; and there was Lorraine, who lived in South Beach, almost an hour away; and there was Vera, the housekeeper, who sometimes was my only contact with humanity for days on end. It would be good to hang out with my sister. She knew me better than anyone in the world.

In April, the strike ended and Jose went off to Fort Myers for late spring training. I flew to Boston to find us a place to live. My sister went with me. We found a beautiful condo overlooking the Charles River, and—like the dutiful girlfriend—I began to get everything organized. I handled the lease, made arrangements with the movers, and scoped out the neighborhood.

When I got back to Florida, Lorraine called. She came to visit, and we ended up taking a little Ecstasy. I got that same wonderful, fuzzy, lovey-dovey feeling, and I guess she did, too, because before long she started kissing me and telling me she thought I was really hot. "I've always been attracted to you," she said.

Under normal circumstances, I wouldn't have let anything happen. But under the influence of drugs, people do strange things. I was a little nervous at first, but Lorraine was so warm and nurturing that I got over my fear. We kissed a little but mostly snuggled and talked. Lorraine treated me with such love and tenderness that I almost wept with gratitude.

Afterward, when we were lying there, snuggling, I remember thinking that—in the space of a few hours—Lorraine had taken care of me in ways that Jose had never managed.

It didn't make any sense. None of it made any sense.

I never told Jose about Lorraine, of course, and I wasn't about to. He had cheated on me so often that in some ways I felt I was paying him back. But that didn't seem entirely accurate. On the one hand, it didn't really feel like cheating. On the other hand, it felt worse than cheating. I had really connected with Lorraine; I know it was, in part, the Ecstasy, but it didn't make it any less real. I had connected with her in ways I had never connected with

Jose, both physically and emotionally. She had been totally *there* for me.

When Jose returned to the house during a break from spring training, he found me in bed, leafing through a pet magazine, with the two cats curled up at my feet. "How's it going?" he asked.

"Let's get another cat," I said.

"If we're going to get another cat, it's got to be something big," he said.

"You mean like those South American cougars I was reading about?"

"Yeah," he said. "Make some calls. Find out how much they are."

Two weeks later, we drove to Plantation, Florida, and picked up a baby cougar from a man who was probably breaking the law. That same man told us about a Siberian lynx that needed a home, and Jose said we might be interested. He asked him to contact us when he had more information.

We were wild about out little cougar. Even Vera fell in love with her. We called her Buffy. She was very playful, very demanding, and followed us everywhere. In an odd way, I began to understand motherhood—you're so busy tending to another living creature that you forget all about yourself.

I was pretty much in charge of Buffy, who needed to be bottle-fed during the first weeks. When she started eating solids, I discovered that she only liked raw chicken liver, ground into mush. The local butcher began setting it aside for me, and he always looked happy to see me.

"How's Buffy?" he'd ask.

"She's doing great."

"And you?"

"Wonderful."

I always got the feeling that he wanted me to stay and chat, but I had to get home to my baby. She ate the raw chicken liver out of my hand.

By this time, the four-acre property was crawling with critters. Jose knew how much I loved animals, and this was one area where he catered to my whims. Most girls wanted flowers. I got iguanas, turtles, birds, and a wild cat. It was Jose's ways of telling me he loved me. It was easier than actually saying it out loud.

The animals tended to keep me at home, which Jose wasn't exactly thrilled about. He would ask me to join him at spring training, but I always begged off. "I can't leave my babies," I said. "They depend on me."

"Vera can take care of them."

"Not Buffy," I said. "Buffy couldn't make it without me."

The animals made me happy. They were a wonderful source of distraction, like shopping and nose jobs. When the time came to go to Boston, however, I knew that I could only take a few of them. Buffy was a given—she needed me—but I also decided to take the two house cats. They weren't cougars, but at least they were in the cat family, and all three of them seemed to get along just fine. Jose paid for an extra seat on the plane, and they all traveled in little cages at our feet.

From the moment we settled into the condo, things got crazy, but *good* crazy. Jose was going off on road trips every other week, and I couldn't go with him because I had the three cats to take care of. Maybe I had planned it that way, consciously or not. I was tired of the constant traveling, and I realized that I only went along to keep Jose from cheating. Now I was too busy to think about his cheating. Well, that's not entirely true. I thought about it, but I had enough distractions at home to make it bearable. And I created other distractions. On weekends, I went Rollerblading with my sister. And when I'd had enough of the cats, I went shopping. Shopping always seemed to work wonders. I had become more style conscious over the years, perhaps because I'd spend so much time around all of those chic baseball wives, and I was up on all the latest fashions. I was wearing leather boots and tank tops, and my hair was long, blonde, and streaked with countless highlights.

One month, just out of curiosity, I tallied up my various receipts: clothes, beauty treatments, more clothes, more beauty treatments. I had managed to spend close to twenty thousand dollars.

When Jose got back from his road trips, he would see the bills and pay them without a word of complaint. When you're making the kind of money he was making, twenty thousand dollars must seem like a drop in the bucket.

Then we got word that the lynx was ready for delivery, and we arranged to have it shipped to the Boston airport. We went to pick it up together, signed for it, and brought it home in its little crate. She was adorable. We called her Libby. She and Buffy got along like two peas in a pod, and for a while the menagerie was very happy. But before long, Libby began to look a little lethargic, and I decided to take her to see a vet. It was a little harder than I expected. None of them wanted to treat a lynx. Finally, in desperation, I mentioned that she belonged to Jose Canseco—and the first vet I spoke to rolled out the red carpet.

The news was grim. The lynx had Feline Immunodeficiency Virus (FIV), also known as Feline AIDS, and she had to be put to sleep. I didn't want to put her to sleep. I asked for a few extra days, took her back to the condo, and I made her final hours on earth as pleasant as I possibly could. I made Jose take her back to the vet's office, and I locked myself in the bedroom and sobbed.

For days afterward I survived by going from one distraction to the next. The shopping bills were considerably higher that month. And I spent a lot of time in the hair salon, changing my look so often it seemed as if I wanted to become another person.

One of the girls at the hair salon was a friend of Niki Taylor, the model/actress, and she told me I should meet Jean Renard, who was Niki's manager, as well as a fashion photographer. "He's always looking for new talent," she said. "You're beautiful. You could have quite a career."

I called Jean and we made arrangements to meet, and he was so full of compliments that he had me blushing. He kept telling me that I was stunning, beautiful, and wonderful, and asked if we could do some pictures. He wanted to start shooting as soon as possible.

I called Jose, and he wasn't happy about it. "Who is this guy?"

"A talent manager, and a very good photographer."

"Photographer? What do you need pictures for?"

"I don't know. I was thinking I could model."

"You're going to leave me now? You're going to be a model?" He was joking around and trying to be cute, but I could see that he was worried. He was threatened by anything that could make me independent. He wanted me at home, with him, always at his beck and call.

"I really want to do this," I said.

"Okay," he said, relenting. "But I want to see the pictures. *All* the pictures."

I don't know what he thought I was up to, but everything I shot with Jean was totally chaste. In those days, I would never have taken my shirt off for a camera. I mean, I didn't even have the courage to enter a wet T-shirt contest.

Jean was very patient with me. He took some head shots and a few shots of me wearing various outfits, and he only had one complaint. "You have to work on your facial expressions," he said. "You need to know when to turn it on for the camera. It's hard work."

"I'm a little tense," I admitted.

"Don't worry. You'll get it. It takes getting used to."

Jean and I started spending time together, shopping for CDs or chatting over coffee, all of it completely innocent. It bugged the hell out of Jose. "I don't like you hanging out with other guys," he said. "It doesn't look right."

I liked Jean, but I didn't want to fight with Jose. I could have told him what I'd already told him a dozen times—that I wasn't like him, that I didn't cheat, that he was projecting. But it wasn't worth it. I decided to protect my relationship, and I called Jean to tell him what was going on. "He's a little upset. He thinks this is going to interfere with our relationship. I'm not sure if I can do this."

He took a moment, weighing what he was about to tell me. "Listen, Jessica, this isn't my business, and I probably have no right saying it, but I'm going to say it anyway. You should stop thinking about the fast cars and the expensive shoes and the money. If you're not happy, and I can see you're not happy, none of it means anything."

"I know," I said.

"You're a smart, talented girl. You don't need him to make you happy."

"That's a lot to think about," I said. "But thank you. I mean it."

"I'm here if you need me," he replied. "*I* mean it."

The irony is that Jean was the type of guy I should have been with: decent, attentive, genuine, and smart. On top of everything, he was trying to get me to believe in myself. But I didn't believe in myself. I had no identity without Jose.

When Jose came back from his next road trip, he asked me to pick him up at Fenway Park. He looked really happy to see me. A little *too* happy. He took me into one of those rooms under the tunnel, pulled up my skirt, and was inside me before I even knew what hit me.

That was some greeting! It made me feel good. If he was that horny, I figured he hadn't cheated on me during that trip. It was also a thrill hearing footsteps moving past the door and thinking we were going to get caught.

Two days later, we were in bed back at the condo when I had an orgasm. I think I was still glowing a little from the quickie at

Fenway Park and was looser than I'd ever been, or maybe I was at my sexual peak at that moment. I don't know. All I know is that Jose happened to hit the spot, and he hit it just right, and I didn't want that feeling to go away. "Yeah," I purred. "Right there." Before I knew it, I had a genuine, earthshaking orgasm. I collapsed on the bed, spent. I finally understood what all the fuss was about! This was better than anything I'd ever experienced. Better than Lorraine. Better than Ecstasy.

"Oh my God," I told Jose, still breathing hard. "That was so good."

He didn't get it. Maybe I'd used that line once or twice before when I was faking it or maybe I was a better actress than I thought, and as a result I always managed to look spent and happy for my man. But this was the real thing, and I wanted to celebrate. How, though? What was I going to say? "You know, Jose—all those other times, I was faking. We've been screwing for more than two years, and this is the first time I've come."

So I let it go, but in the days and weeks that followed our sex life improved by leaps and bounds. I began to take more responsibility for my body. I shifted from one position to the next, until it felt just right. I was more controlling. If I wanted to be on top, I didn't ask—I got on top. And if I wanted to be on my side, with him behind me, that's where I put myself. I even learned to tell Jose how to touch me, which is a delicate proposition under the best of circumstances. Men hate to feel that they're doing anything wrong.

After that, things got very liberal. I took an interest in Jose's porn collection. We went to specialty stores and bought toys: vibrators, dildos, creams, and oils.

The next time Jose went on the road, I went with him. He packed the steroids into his suitcase, and I packed the sex toys into mine. We had so much sex that I knew Jose couldn't possibly be cheating on me, but when we got back to Boston, I discovered I was wrong. Jose gave me another bacterial infection.

The doctor didn't want to implicate Jose. "It's hard to tell what it is," he said. "Have you been having a lot of sex? Sometimes you can get these types of infections from too much sex."

I wondered if a female doctor would have agreed. I wondered if Jose called ahead and asked the doctor to protect him.

"Bend over," I said. We were back at the condo. It was time for Jose's shot. I was playing Nurse Jessica again. I stuck the needle in his rump and pumped him up.

I went along on Jose's next trip, to Baltimore, to keep an eye on him, and my sister and her husband agreed to take care of the cats. She loved the cats.

The night we arrived in Baltimore, I saw one of the other players—a married player—walking through the hotel lobby with a voluptuous little groupie. I knew his wife, vaguely, and I kind of liked her, and I wondered how I was going to break it to her when I got back to Boston. Then I remembered the unwritten code. It hung over me like a threat. If I said anything, it would create problems. For me. For Jose. For the player and his wife. For the team.

"How many times do I have to tell you?" Jose said, scolding me. "You don't say a word." Then he told me that Esther had once ratted out a fellow player and that the player and Jose had almost come to blows. "It's a miracle we didn't kill each other," he said.

Okay. Fine. Live by the code; die by the code. *Voluptuous little groupie?* I don't know what you're talking about. I didn't see a thing.

It made me feel bad, though. I felt spineless. I didn't have any courage at all. And as far as I could tell, the code of silence only served one purpose: to let the players cheat with impunity.

When the 1995 season ended, we took our three cats and went back to the big house in Weston. Jose had not had a great season. He had home runs in five straight games in late August, but he'd had problems with his groin, rib cage, and elbow, and he had spent several weeks on the disabled list. I think he was as tired as I'd ever seen him, which may have had something to do with his announcement, which caught me by surprise: "I think we should have a baby," he said.

"What?"

"You heard me. I'm thirty-two years old. You're twenty-three. We should have a baby."

It was typical Jose. It had nothing to do with his feelings for me or with his desire to make me an honest woman. It was either connected to the fact that Ozzie and Amy had just had a baby or to his own sense of mortality. I thought it was a little early to talk about mortality, but the idea of having a baby grew on me for other reasons. I thought it would change Jose, and in a way I was right: The change was almost instant. To develop viable sperm, he had to lay off the steroids, so from one day to the next he stopped taking them.

"You're supposed to taper off slowly," I told him. He knew it too—it was important to let the body readjust to its own production rhythms—but he didn't give a damn. "I'm going to go cold turkey."

It turned into the worst off-season of my life. Jose just sat in a chair, depressed most of the time. There was no life in him. The few times we had sex, it was only because I insisted; he seemed to be going through the motions against his will. I didn't want him on steroids and had often warned him about the long-term effects, but suddenly I began to reconsider. I thought if he took another shot or two it would boost his spirits, but he wouldn't listen. He said he knew what he was doing. "It's just a matter of time," he assured me.

Within a few weeks, as his battered body adjusted to the absence of drugs, he began to emerge from his depression, even signing a new two-year contract with the Boston Red Sox for $8.95 million. But there was still very little life in him, and he remained only marginally interested in sex. I noticed that his balls were slowly beginning to look like regular-sized ones. His penis, however, had lost some of its girth. And he had a tough time keeping it hard. It embarrassed him. It made him even less interested in sex. The only upside was that I no longer worried about him cheating on me. He was around all the time, looking sad and dejected. If he did go out, it was only to play an occasional round of golf with his brother.

One day, I came home to find that Buffy had chewed her way through part of the leather couch. By the time Jose returned to the house, I'd managed to have it carted away. Jose noticed immediately, which was something of a surprise. "Where's the sofa?" he asked.

"What sofa?"

"Okay," he said, smiling. "Tell me what Buffy did."

We realized we had to give up Buffy. We found a wild animal sanctuary a few hours from the house in Northern Florida and made arrangements with the owners. I wept all the way home. But I went to visit every few weeks, and Buffy always looked happy to see me.

There was a lesson in all this: Don't buy animals that you can't legally own.

When Christmas rolled around, Ozzie and Amy came to visit with the baby, and Jose thought it was the cutest thing he had ever seen. He repeated that he wanted a baby, and this time I actually addressed the issue. "You want a baby, but you won't talk about engagement or marriage?"

"I had a bad marriage. It scares me."

"I'm not Esther," I said.

"I just want a family," he said.

"So do I," I said. "If you want a family, it's a good idea to get married first. I'm not interested in just having a baby. If you should be scared of anything, it's of the responsibility that comes from having a baby."

"I know."

"We could get engaged," I suggested.

"Yeah, we could." He didn't say it with much energy. I could see he wasn't ready for that commitment, but at least he seemed to be thinking about it.

One morning, shortly before Christmas, he sauntered over with his diamond pinky ring. He hadn't worn it in a while. "Why don't we turn this into an engagement ring?" he asked. It wasn't exactly the most romantic moment in my life, but the four karats made it easier to bear. A few days later, we visited a local jewelry store and picked out the band, and they got to work setting the stone. Jose showed absolutely no emotion at all. We may as well have been shopping for cat food.

Christmas came and went, and I was so annoyed by Jose's lethargy and depression that I again urged him to get back on steroids. He didn't talk at all now, and in fact didn't even seem to be aware that I existed. *Hello! I'm over here! Remember me? I think we just got engaged!* I got absolutely nothing from him, and it began to crush me.

Sometimes I tried humor. I would dance around in my tap shoes and underwear, trying to get a laugh out of him, but even that didn't work. And I look pretty good in tap shoes and underwear.

To make matters worse, I had no friends. Vera was busy trying to keep the huge house in order, and Jose was too cheap to hire more help. Amy had gone off to Jacksonville to stay with her sisters. She had the baby, and her marriage to Ozzie was already falling apart.

"He never talks to me, and when he's around the house, all he does is mope," she told me when we first spoke on the phone. "I get the feeling that he's cheating on me." She didn't sound very hopeful about the situation.

"Sounds just like Jose," I said.

"Yeah," she said dejectedly. "The Fabulous Canseco Brothers."

Ozzie would come to Weston to visit, and he had his own interpretation. "Amy's crazy," he'd tell us. "She's losing her mind. She thinks I'm cheating on her. Can you believe that? *Me? Cheating?*"

I'll reserve comment on the cheating part, but the rest of it sounded oddly familiar. It seemed that both Canseco brothers had hooked up with crazy women.

Later, after Ozzie had gone home, Jose would tell me, "My brother is very difficult to live with. You're lucky. I'm not like him at all." Then he would get back to badgering me about having a baby. "Man! Look at you! You're a good breeder!"

"I don't know what you mean," I said. "I've never bred anything in my life."

"I'm talking about your genes. We could make a real beautiful baby."

I pointed out that we had to have sex to make a baby, and I managed to get him into bed and bring him back to life, albeit briefly. After sex, I remember standing on my head to improve our chances of getting pregnant. "See!" I said, trying to get a laugh out of him. "Maybe your sperm are slow. Or maybe they're still half-dead from all the 'roids. They're going to need a lot of help finding their way. Maybe this will do it. We all have to do our part."

Despite the stabs at humor, I was conflicted about this whole baby thing. I wanted one, and I wanted us to be a family, but I also wanted the old Jose back. There was more than a little irony in this: The old Jose hadn't been all that wonderful, but he was better than the one I had now.

By February 1996, Jose reached the end of his rope. "Screw

this," he said. "I don't feel good, and I don't look good. I'm going back on steroids. Baseball's starting up."

I almost felt like cheering. How pathetic is that? "What about the baby?" I asked.

"Maybe next year," he said. "But I can't go on like this. It's going to kill my career."

Nurse Jessica got back to work. We had sex again, *good* sex, and a few days later he had to fly to Texas on baseball-related business. Or so he said. The following morning, I found a Texas phone number in his pants pocket. My bullshit detector kicked in, and I called it.

The number belonged to a stripper. Jose was back in fighting form.

When I called to confront him, he denied it, and blamed it on a friend of his, but at this point I'd had enough. "It's never going to end," I said, feeling drained and defeated. "You're always cheating on me. I can't make you happy. I'm tired of killing myself to make this work when you don't want it to work."

"Jessica, don't say that!" he protested. "You know it's not true!"

"It is true. All these years, I've been living my life for you. Everything is about Jose. I'm a person, too, you know. I have feelings, too. And you're breaking my heart. I don't understand why I'm not enough for you."

"Jessica, listen to me—"

"No, I'm done listening."

I hung up, very proud of myself, and I went out and got the newspaper and started looking through the real estate section.

Jose called and called, but I wouldn't answer the phone. The next day I went to look at apartments, and I found a cute little place in Miami Beach. I signed the lease and put down a deposit: first month, last month, and security.

I felt strong, independent, and empowered by my actions. Then Jose came home and the strength seeped out of me. We made love. It was nice. My addiction to him had kicked back in, stronger than ever.

"You look skinny," he said.

"I'm stressed," I said.

"And your skin's breaking out."

"Thanks," I said. "You make me feel so beautiful."

"Don't leave, Jessica. Please. We could be happy together."

"Could we?"

"Yeah. But first you need to gain a little weight."

"I know. I'm so tired lately. Maybe I should be doing steroids."

Jose seemed suddenly enthused. "Yeah," he said. "Winstrol would do wonders for you."

"I wasn't serious," I said.

"No," he said. "It's a good idea. Winstrol's good for energy. And it gives you appetite. We should do this."

I thought about it. It couldn't hurt, right? I felt skinny, ugly, and completely listless. I felt like Jose looked when he got off the steroids. Maybe he had a point. A little shot in the rump might set things right. After all, it had turned him around almost instantly.

"I don't want to look like a muscled freak," I said.

"You won't. Trust me. I know what I'm doing."

I finally caved, but it took hours before I let him give me the shot. I was scared. I have hated needles all my life, and I was breaking into a sweat. Finally, I let him do it, and I screamed so loud that Vera came running. Jose sent her on her way and told her everything was fine. But it wasn't fine. The muscle in my ass was killing me. For the next three days, I was dragging my leg behind me as I made my way around the house. I felt like a character in a bad comedy.

That weekend, he said he had to do it again. One shot wasn't going to do the trick. I cried and screamed, but finally I gave in and he shot up my other cheek. It was even worse than the first time. I couldn't understand how Jose had withstood that kind of pain on such a regular basis over the course of so many years. "I am never doing this again," I said.

I felt unusually irritable for a few days and wondered whether it was because of the steroids. But when that passed, and when my ass had recovered, I went furniture shopping for my new apartment. He was hurt, but he kept his anger in check. "I can't believe you're still thinking of moving out," he said. "I thought we were doing good."

"Three days without an argument is not 'doing good,' " I said.

"Come with me to spring training," he said. He was getting ready for his second season with the Red Sox, and he was on his way to Fort Myers for the first leg of the season. "I promise everything's going to be great."

"No," I said. "I need some time to think."

"But you're not moving out, right?"

"I don't know." I really didn't know. All I knew is that I

couldn't break away from him when he was physically present. I needed him gone. That was my only chance.

The day he left for spring training he got all emotional. "Give me one last chance, baby. Please. I'm sorry. You're more than enough for me. I love you. You're my girl."

I didn't say anything. I didn't want to be weak.

"Just say maybe," he said. "Say you'll think about it."

"I'll think about it," I said, sounding a little like a robot.

"I love you, Jessica. You know that."

He took off, and I decided I absolutely had to go through with the move. I began to pack my things. I arranged for the furniture to be delivered to my new apartment.

Jose called me the next day. "Did you think about what I said?"

"I'm moving out, Jose."

"Don't say that. What are you going to do?"

"I don't know. I think I'm going to try modeling. I'm going to start putting a portfolio together."

"You know how long that's going to take?"

"I don't care. I have to start somewhere."

"Jesus Christ, Jessica. You're fucking me up! I'm trying to play ball here, and you say you're leaving me and I can't goddamn focus!" I didn't say anything, so he went on: "I'm *not* cheating on you. Leave it alone. Why can't you be good to me?"

The conversation went on for a few minutes before he was called away and hung up, still seething. I picked up the phone and called Jean Renard in Boston. I think Jose's poor choice of words had fueled my strength. *Why can't you be good to me?* Was he nuts? I'd been nothing but good.

When Jean answered the phone, I told him I was ready to get on with my career.

"How does Jose feel about it?" he asked.

"I don't care," I said. "I'm moving out. I just got an apartment in Miami, and I'm ready to move forward."

Two days later, I flew to Boston and went to stay with my sister and her husband. The next day, I went to see Jean. He thought I looked a little muscular, and he wasn't wrong. The steroids had kicked in. In less than two weeks, thanks to the Chemist, I'd gained five or six pounds of pure muscle.

"You've been working out," Renard noted.

"Yes," I said. I didn't think I should mention the 'roids.

"Cut back on it," he said. "It doesn't look good on film."

Jean had set a few hours aside, and we spent the time shooting and talking. He said he was very proud of me. He said a lot of women in similar situations had a difficult time finding the courage to break free.

I felt really good about myself. For the first time in my life, I really felt I was going somewhere. I was going to take care of myself, and I was going to succeed. I actually felt wildly optimistic. It occurred to me that true happiness comes from true freedom. I didn't want Jose anymore. I didn't want that lifestyle. I didn't want all that *stuff*. It was just stuff, after all; I was better than that, and I deserved better than that. I was finally coming to terms with the total lack of meaning in my life. Lamborghinis are nice, but any schmuck with money can drive one. It doesn't speak to who you are as a human being, and it doesn't make you happy. And if it gets you places faster, it only gives you that much more time to think about how little it really means.

When I got back to the house in Weston, the phone was ringing. It was Jose. He was still at spring training. "I want to be with you," he said. "I love you. Don't do this to us. I'm not going to make it without you."

If he'd been standing in front of me, with tears in his eyes, I probably couldn't have pulled myself together. But he was hundreds of miles away, just a voice on the telephone. "No," I said. "You don't understand. I need to do this for me. I have to start thinking about me."

"What about the animals?"

What animals? The cougar was gone. The lynx was dead. The two house cats were totally independent. And the rest of the menagerie—the turtles, birds, and iguanas—couldn't tell one human being from another. All they cared about was being fed, not who did the feeding. "The animals will be fine," I said. "Vera's here. I'll come over and look in on them from time to time."

"You're really fucking me up," Jose said, his voice cracking with emotion.

"That makes two of us," I said, and I hung up.

I was proud of myself and of my strength, but the minute I got off the phone I started to cry. And I couldn't stop. I cried for hours. On the inside I was happy—I was finally breaking free—but my tears told a different story. I thought I was going crazy. I didn't know what to feel. I tried to rationalize it. I told myself it was okay to feel confused and unhinged. I had actually done it. I was moving out. In a matter of days, my new furniture would be arriving in my new apartment, and I would start my new life. Of course I felt a little crazy! This was a monumental, life-changing experience. Only a truly crazy person could have gotten through it without feeling wildly off balance.

And that's when it hit me. My period was late. I raced to the local pharmacy and bought a pregnancy test and put myself through several minutes of sheer hell. It came up positive. I didn't know what to do. I ran downstairs, looking for Vera. "I'm pregnant!" I said. "I'm pregnant!"

Vera practically started crying. She threw her arms around me and gave me a big hug. "So you're not leaving!" she said. She was over the moon.

"I don't know," I said. "Maybe the test is wrong."

We went down to Planned Parenthood together, me and a fifty-year-old housekeeper, and I took a blood test. "Mr. Canseco is going to be very happy," she said as we waited for the results. "Mr. Canseco wants a baby. A baby is a good thing for a man like him. He'll change. You'll see. He loves you."

A few minutes later, the nurse returned with the results. "It's positive," she said. "You are definitely pregnant."

CHAPTER 9

Having My Baby

As it turned out, I was farther along than I thought. I had missed two periods, not one, but the first one hadn't registered because that was the week I did those two shots of steroids. Suddenly I went into a panic. I called the doctor and told him that I'd done steroids right around the time I became pregnant. He told me not to worry. He explained that at that stage the embryo was about the size of a fingernail, and it was highly unlikely there would have been any ill effects at all.

When I got off the phone, I didn't know what to think. I was pregnant. I couldn't leave Jose now. What was I going to do about my new apartment? My new furniture? My new career? My new *life*?

I called my mother, back in Ohio. "Mom, are you sitting down? I'm pregnant."

"Pregnant?! Really? I can't believe it!"

"Believe it," I said.

"What can I do, Jess? You want me to come visit? You want to come home for a few days? How can I help?"

"I don't know," I said. And I didn't. I wanted to be more excited about being pregnant, but I was worried about Jose.

Then again, maybe Vera was right; maybe Jose *would* change.

A baby would be good for Mr. Canseco, she had told me. Now I thought a baby would be good for us both. We would be a family. We would be happy.

Or would we?

I was vacillating between one extreme and the other. I didn't know whether to be happy or sad. I thought I was kidding myself. Jose would never change. We'd never be happy.

I finally called him. "Guess what?" I said. "I'm pregnant."

"Oh my God! Are you sure?"

"Yes. I'm six weeks along."

"Wow," he said. "I can't believe it. He started singing: "'Having my baby. What a lovely way of saying how much you love me.'"

"This isn't funny, Jose. I'm not sure what I want to do."

"Well, you can't leave me now," he said.

"Why not? You honestly think this is going to change things for the better?"

"What's that supposed to mean?" he asked. "Don't tell me you're thinking of having an abortion?"

"I don't know what I'm thinking," I said. "I've never been so confused in my life."

"That means it's not mine!"

"What are you talking about?!"

"If it was mine, you wouldn't be thinking about having an abortion!"

"For God's sake, Jose—how can you even say that to me?!"

"You went to Boston!"

"I'm not like you! I haven't been with anyone!"

"Why would you want to kill our baby?!" he asked.

"Stop it!" I said. "We're both going crazy here!"

"Please don't kill our baby, Jessica."

"I'm not. I'm just, you know—a baby's a big thing. I don't think you really understand that, Jose. And I'm the one who's having it, so it's an even bigger thing for me."

"So you're having it?"

"Well, I don't particularly want to have an abortion."

"That's good," he said. "We can be a family now. Just like I said. Just what I wanted."

It was amazing to me. That's all he ever thought about—Jose. As far as he was concerned, the timing couldn't have been better. I wasn't leaving him, he could focus on baseball, and he was getting what he wanted. Plus now he could go back to fucking around. I wondered if he had his eye on a special girl for that very evening.

"I'm so happy, Jessica. You've made me a happy man. Come to Fort Myers."

He was a happy man, but what about me? Did he ask? Did he care?

I packed my stuff. Vera helped me. She kept telling me how happy *she* was. Everyone was happy, it seemed, except me. And the funny thing is that I wasn't unhappy about being pregnant. Not at all. The notion of having a baby growing inside me was wonderful and exciting and even a little frightening (in a good way). The unhappiness stemmed from my doubts about Jose. I had come so close to escaping him, and it seemed as if fate were pulling me right back.

When I arrived at the hotel in Fort Myers, Jose was beaming. What is it about men and pregnancy? They begin to strut around like they have huge dicks. "Did I tell you how happy I am, baby?" he kept asking.

"A few times," I said.

"Why do you look so pale?"

Instead of answering, I got off the bed and hurried into the bathroom and promptly threw up. For the next few days, I had terrible morning sickness. At one point, lying in bed, groaning, I called Jean Renard in Boston.

"Hey," I squawked. "It's me. Jessica."

"Jessica," he said. "I've been trying to reach you! Some of these shots turned out great."

"I'm pregnant," I said.

There was a long pause. "Really?" he asked. "What are you going to do?"

"I don't know. Have the baby."

"Are you happy?"

I was "happy" with reservations. I was happy and a little afraid.

"I'm not sure," I said. "It hasn't sunk in yet."

A few nights later, Jose got back to the room and seemed a little skittish. He undressed and took a shower, and as he dried himself off he told me he was going out to have a beer with some of the guys. "You okay with room service?" he asked.

"Sure," I said. I'd been living on room service. My life was waiters in white jackets bringing me food.

The moment Jose left, I knew something wasn't right. Jose

didn't hang out with *the guys.* When Jose went out, it was generally about women.

I began to call some strip clubs near the hotel. I acted like a sweet little groupie. "Is Jose Canseco there?" I would ask. The first two places said he wasn't there. But when I reached the third place, they told me he had just left.

I called my mother and vented, thinking I would pack up and leave. But by the end of the conversation, I'd had a change of heart. Where was I going to go? I was pregnant and unmarried. Leaving wasn't even an option. I was going to stay, have the baby, and work hard at turning us into a real family. When Jose saw the baby, how could he not change?

The next morning, I called Miami and broke my lease. They had no problem with it, but they were going to keep my entire deposit. The furniture people were somewhat more understanding, but they still charged me an exorbitant restocking fee.

Then we went off to Boston: Jose and his pregnant fiancée. I felt and looked awful. I had no energy. My face was breaking out. I remember going to a local doctor and whining, "Can't you at least fix my face?" The answer was no. It was hormonal. There was nothing he could do.

To make matters worse, I didn't even have my sister anymore. She and her husband had moved to Rochester, New York. I spoke to her on the phone from time to time, and I spoke to my mother, but after a while I got tired of hearing myself whine.

The only good news had nothing to do with me. The Red Sox were having a good year, and Jose was part of it. Sometimes he'd come home in a great mood and find me in bed, watching TV, looking morose. It was as if we had switched roles. He would sit down next to me and rub my belly. "How're my girls?" he'd ask, and more often than not I would burst into tears and turn my back. "Jessica, baby, what's wrong? You want to talk about it?"

"No."

We had switched roles in more ways than one. Now he was the one who wanted to talk, while I preferred not to. I didn't know what we could possibly talk about. I was sure I wanted the baby, but not so sure I wanted the man. But did I want to be an unwed mother? And was it wise to have the baby if the man wasn't worth keeping?

I went to visit my sister in Rochester and tried to keep the whining and crying to a minimum. Late that evening, exhausted, I decided to call Jose. I reached him on his cell phone, and it was so noisy I could hardly hear. There was loud music and lots of laughter, and most of the laughter was distinctly female. "What's going on?" I asked.

"My brother's visiting," he said.

"So you're having a party?"

"No," he said. "Just a few people."

Then I heard a woman's voice, and it was so clear and unmistakable that I knew exactly what that horrible bitch was up to: "Jose! Come have a drink!"

A split second later the call ended. He hung up on me, knowing I had heard the girl's voice. I was heartbroken. I knew I hadn't misheard. I imagined the scene: Jose, Ozzie, and a bunch of players partying in one of the suites, surrounded by a bunch of half-naked groupies, every last one of them aching to serve. It killed me. I slinked off into the bedroom and wept, and there was nothing my sister could do to console me. "He's never going to change," I said between sobs. "I can't believe I fell for that shameless bastard."

I kept calling and calling and calling Jose's cell, but he wouldn't answer. When I finally got through, hours later, he told me his phone wasn't working properly. I didn't even register his pathetic lies about his cell phone not working. I was more concerned about that bitch. "I wasn't with anybody, Jessica!" he said. "She was talking to one of the other players!"

"How many Joses were in the room with you?"

"What do I have to do to convince you?"

He convinced me all right. He convinced me he was lying. Two weeks later, after we'd kissed and made up, I was back at the doctor with another bacterial infection. I'd had enough self-denial to last me a lifetime. This wasn't something you got from towels. Or toilet seats. Or by having pretty girls sneeze in your general direction.

"I have a life growing inside me!" I screamed at Jose. "This could be bad for the baby!"

"I thought the doctor took care of it."

"He did! That's not the point. The point is you're sleeping around!"

"I'm not! I told you. If you want me to say I'm sorry, I'll say I'm sorry. But I'm not sleeping around!"

I called my sister for advice, but she was reluctant to say anything, one way or another. She knew I was in pretty deep, what with the baby and everything. "I don't know what to tell you," she said. "It's who he is. You may not want to hear that, and it probably makes you sad, but that's all I can tell you. That's who Jose is." She was trying to be supportive.

My mother was less cautious. "Doesn't he realize how important this is? You're going to have a baby. The kind of life he leads is not going to be good for the baby."

It wasn't going to be good for the baby, and it wasn't going to be good for me, but at this point there was no turning back, so I decided to move forward. "What about getting married?" I asked Jose.

"I thought we'd wait a year or so," he said.

"Yes," I said. "That was the original plan, when we got engaged, and you haven't said anything since. But now we have the baby to worry about. If nothing else, think about health insurance."

"You've got a point," he said. "Let's get married in September, when the season ends."

"I'll be huge by September."

"Don't worry about it," he said. "That'll just be for legal purposes. We'll have a nice big wedding after the baby's born."

I believed him.

Then he ruptured a disc. He took a swing at the ball, twisting his back, and on August 1 he was placed on the disabled list—for back surgery. Jose was understandably upset. Still, with twenty-eight home runs in only four months, it hadn't been a bad season.

He underwent surgery in Boston, and I was by his side, the dutiful fiancée, waiting in his hospital room for him to wake up. I fell asleep on a chair near the bed, watching the morphine drip into his body. I could have used a little morphine myself. I wondered if they had morphine for the soul. The closest I'd ever come was Ecstasy and that had been a long time ago. With motherhood looming, I knew my rolling days were over. Right?

When Jose was well enough to travel, we went back to the house in Weston so he could recover. The season was over for him. We were a pathetic couple. I was getting bigger and slower, and he was limping around like an injured soldier.

Now that we were home, we decided to move the wedding up. That August, we had a little civil ceremony at the house. We were to be married by his attorney, with his family and a few friends in attendance. But just before we were about to begin, Jose said his back was killing him. We went up to the bedroom and Jose lay down on our big bed. I was wearing a simple white dress. I lay down next to him. The attorney said a few words, which I didn't quite catch, and pronounced us man and wife. It wasn't exactly the wedding I had dreamed about as a little girl. Jose was marrying me for insurance purposes. How romantic. Still, he assured me that we'd have a proper wedding after the baby arrived—the wedding I deserved.

At least we weren't fighting anymore. I think we were both too tired to fight. We slipped into a quiet life, the days running effortlessly into one another. We'd watch TV, eat, sleep, cool off in the pool, and sleep some more. I still read a lot, books about motherhood, health and fitness, and true crime, but I could no longer read while on the floor of my big walk-in closet. My pregnancy had cost me my sanctuary. The only plus side to being pregnant was eating. I ate like a pig. I had a baby to feed.

When Jose started feeling better, he decided to play handyman. He had this bright idea that he should build a giant cage for the iguanas, made of thick, Plexiglas and he got to work on it. He was out there every day for a month, and every day it looked worse and worse. The iguanas wouldn't go near it. One day, one of them climbed on the roof and Jose couldn't go after it because of his bad back, so I went, despite my huge belly. It was actually kind of funny. I rested the iguana on my big belly and cooed at it, a mother in training.

On September 27, 1996, Barry Bonds became the first player to match Jose's record, with forty homers and forty steals. If Jose had any feelings about it—one way or another—he didn't share them with me.

We went out and bought things for the baby. The room was ready—the previous owners had a child—so all we had to do was stock it. Sheets, pillows, diapers, blankies, and baby wipes.

Jose's family gave me a baby shower. I was smiling on the outside, but I was more terrified than ever on the inside. Jose, however, appeared quite happy. He seemed to be looking forward to fatherhood. For a few weeks, he was attentive and available. When his back improved, he went out to play a little golf from time to time, but he was always reachable on his cell, and I never heard any women in the background.

One day he told me he was going to the gym for rehab. This was the first I'd heard of it, and I wondered why he didn't work out at the gym on the property. He could have hired someone to help him out in the comfort of his own home. I didn't question him, though. Things had been moving along nicely, and I didn't want to rock the boat again.

"Stay close," I said. "I'm about ready to pop."

He kissed me good-bye and left, and about half an hour later, as I was in bed feeling my little girl kick, I got a horrible, sinking feeling. I called the gym and found out he'd never shown up. "Are you sure?" I asked.

"Yes, ma'am. He would have signed in. And when Jose's around, we notice."

I called his cell phone, and he didn't answer, so I waited for him to come home. When I heard him pulling into the driveway, I went downstairs to greet him. I was smiling brightly. "Hi honey," I said. "Did you have a nice workout?"

"It was pretty good," he replied. "I took it slow."

"What'd you do?"

"Oh, you know. A little upper-body work."

Upper-body work my ass. Whose body?

"Really?" I asked, beginning to drop the act. "That's very funny because I called the gym, and they said you weren't there."

"What gym did you call?"

"Your regular gym, Jose. The one you go to."

"I went to a different gym today. They had this trainer there—"

"Why don't you just cut the crap, Jose? Where were you?"

He took a deep breath and looked at me. "I was in Miami," he said finally.

"Yeah?"

"I went to see Esther."

"You went to see Esther?"

"I don't know if you knew. Esther just had a baby, on her

own. She was upset, and she called me. She said she wanted to talk. She was crying."

"Oh. I see. Your ex-wife was crying, so you went to comfort her."

"It was nothing, Jessica."

"What did she want to talk about?"

"She said she wanted to get back together."

My jaw dropped. Even if this was true, I didn't think it was a great idea for Jose to share it with his pregnant wife. "She wants to get back together?" I repeated robotically.

"She always says that. She's just sad because she doesn't have a father for her baby."

"Oh? And I suppose she wants you to be the father?" I asked.

"Jessica, why don't we just drop it? I'm not going anywhere. I've got you, and I've got the baby, and everything's fine, okay?"

It didn't feel fine, but I didn't want to push. Jose seemed very sad all of a sudden. Sad, tired, and confused. When we went to bed that night, I could see he was in a very dark place.

"You want to talk about it?" I asked him.

"Not really," he said, and he turned his back and went to sleep.

Our baby was due October 27, and when October 31 came I was feeling pretty anxious. I spoke to the doctor, and he said they'd induce on November 4. I liked that. My birthday was on December 4, so it made for some nice symmetry. I got off the phone and told Jose, but he informed me that we couldn't do it on the fourth. "I've got a game on the fourth," he explained. "Do it on the fifth."

I couldn't believe it. This was a stupid, coed softball game with a bunch of friends, and he was telling me to reschedule so that he wouldn't miss his silly game. "Can't you skip it for once?" I asked.

"No," he replied. "Can't you put it off one more day?"

The good little wife put it off one more day, and Josie Marie Canseco—named for the two of us, a combination of Jose and Jessie—came into the world on November 5, 1996.

My mother and Jose were in the delivery room, but I had asked Jose's side of the family to wait outside. They had all begged to be part of it, but the idea of all of these people cheering me on while I lay spread eagled on the delivery table didn't really appeal to me.

When it was time to begin pushing, I was inexplicably tired. I had barely moved. Of course, that may well have been the reason I was so tired. "Wake up," Jose said. "You have to push. The doctor says you're dilated."

"No," I said. "Let me sleep."

"Baby, it's time to push," Jose said. He was holding my leg, rubbing it, and leaning over my privates. "The baby's ready."

So I pushed, and Josie was out in twelve minutes. I was strong, and I was determined. And I was vain enough to know that I wasn't going to have a Caesarean section.

My mom was crying. Jose was crying. I was crying. Then I heard Josie crying, and I was crying and laughing at the same time. She weighed seven pounds eleven ounces, and she looked absolutely beautiful.

I spent only one night in the hospital, and when we got home, I didn't want anyone near my baby. I was like a she-wolf, baring my teeth at interlopers. Thank God my mother was around. Everyone else was forced to keep their distance. My bond with my daughter was instant and intense. I couldn't believe that this gorgeous little creature had come from me. I would stare at her for hours on end. We'd sit out by the pool, in the shade, watching the iguanas slink past, and if they got too close, I'd bare my teeth at them, too.

My mother helped me understand Josie's needs. One cry was for hunger; another meant she needed to be changed. There were a number of variations on the crying theme, and sometimes neither of us could figure them out, but if I held and rocked her, she would usually quiet down and go to sleep. I refused to leave my baby for a second, and my mother was always hovering at my side, ready to help out at a moment's notice. I felt she was making up for some of those disconnected years.

Jose was as clueless about the baby as he was about my needs. He'd come in and rub her little head and make goo-goo eyes at her, but when it came to making himself useful—changing a diaper, maybe—he suddenly had things to do.

"I've got to finish building the cage for the iguanas," he'd say.

At night, Josie slept in bed between us. I wanted her next to me, where I could hear her breathe, and I wasn't taking any chances with that fancy crib. Jose didn't like it. He hated having to scoot way over to his side of the bed, while his wife and his baby cuddled at the other end. And he wanted sex. I was looking much better, if not exactly hot. It took me only three weeks to get back into fighting shape. I had worked out throughout the pregnancy, and I hadn't gained that much weight, and four days after

I brought Josie home I was in the home gym, with Josie asleep in her bassinet nearby. The pounds just melted away; the muscle returned. Vanity is a great motivator.

One afternoon, Jose got a call from *Selecta,* a Spanish-language magazine. They wanted to do an article on the family. A reporter and photographer came over and made a fuss over the baby, though I kept them at arm's length, too. They took plenty of pictures, and asked Jose a few questions in Spanish. Several weeks later, the magazine was on the stands, featuring Jose Canseco and his perfect family. The article described Jose as a changed man. He'd been whoring around for many years, but the bad boy of baseball had finally settled down.

It was bullshit. He was already cheating on me. I could smell it on him.

Exactly one month after Josie was born, he said he wanted to go to the Bahamas.

"I can't leave Josie!" I said.

"Vera and your mother are here. What's going to happen? We'll hire someone else. You can do that thing where you pump milk."

"I'll worry about her all the time."

"She'll be fine. She's a newborn. Nothing's going to happen. And you can call Vera every day."

"Are you sure she'll be okay?"

"*Yes.* And you'll be okay, too. You need to take a break from time to time."

He was telling me to think about *him,* but he stopped short of spelling it out. Still, I was scared not to go. I was more scared of losing Jose than I'd ever been. That seemed to be the only thing that had changed in the relationship: the panic. I needed him more than ever. I had a baby to worry about.

So we went to the Bahamas, and I called the house three times a day. Everything was fine, of course. And even though I was upset, I managed to have a little fun. We gambled, had a few drinks, made love, and bonded.

"Thank you," I told Jose, snuggling up one night after making love.

"For what?"

"For making me do this. It was a good idea."

It *was* a good idea.

When we got home, I settled back in with my baby, and for a few days I kept apologizing to her for having left. I told her I was back and that it wouldn't happen again. My mother returned to her life in Ohio, and we tried to get on with our lives, or this new version of our lives.

Jose began to spend a lot of time in the huge home gym, inviting friends and family over to work out with him. The place had a terrific weight room, as well as a full-size basketball court. When the gang was done working out and playing, they would hang out by the pool and discuss what they'd just been through. How much so-and-so had lifted. Who had scored the winning point. Fascinating stuff. Snore.

If I asked Jose for help, he told me to ask Vera. "That's what she's there for," he said. He loved Josie, but he wasn't that good at being a dad. He did like showing her off, though. People would look at him with little Josie in his arms, beaming, and they must have thought he was a terrific father. I could have told them different, but I bit my tongue. He loved her, yes, but he had no real clue about parenting.

At night, he and his friends were up till all hours, drinking and playing dominoes. They played Cuban-style dominoes, slamming the tiles against the table and making them sound like gunshots. I would ask him to please keep it down. "I'm trying to get Josie to sleep," I would say. "It's two o'clock in the morning."

"She doesn't know that," he said. "And what difference does it make to her? She's a baby. If she's tired, she can sleep as late as she wants. It's not like she's got a job to go to."

"A baby needs a schedule," I explained, but he didn't give a shit. He went back to join his friends.

At the end of one particularly bad week, I began to wonder what was wrong with me. At the time, I didn't know anything about postpartum depression, but I was always exhausted, constantly worried about my daughter's well-being, and began to doubt my ability to be a good mother. I kept thinking that Josie deserved better. To make matters worse, I began to suspect that I'd made a mistake by having her, not on her account, of course—I was absolutely, hopelessly in love with her—but on Jose's. I didn't think he would make a good father, and somehow this was my fault, too. I had fucked everything up.

But Josie needed me—that was a given. She couldn't survive without me. I had to pull myself together for my daughter. I would endure anything for her, even this horrible depression. If I had known better, I would have sought professional help. I didn't realize it was okay to be unhappy, especially when I had so many reasons to be unhappy.

Jose, meanwhile, remained oblivious. I was a complete wreck—I was back to locking myself in the bathroom, muting my sobs—but he either didn't notice or didn't care. Maybe it was a combination of the two.

Then he decided he was tired of being locked up in the house. He wanted to go to Miami, to party. I was under the impression that we had left Miami, in part, to get away from the partying, but I guess I was wrong. He wanted me to go with him, and I went because I was afraid not to. There was no shortage of beautiful women in South Beach, and Jose was a magnet. I didn't want him to stray.

It was crazy. We would go out for drinks and dinner two or three nights a week, leaving Josie with Vera. I told myself I was doing it for Jose, as if that somehow justified my long absences. We were out late and usually slept beyond noon, and Vera slowly began to take over. She was great with Josie. She'd puree vegetables for her, feed her, and spend the bulk of the day entertaining her. Then I'd drag my tired ass out of bed and go look for my little girl. A perfect mother—not.

On January 27, 1997, Jose got traded back to Oakland. I didn't want to go to Oakland. I didn't want to move again and deal with a whole new set of baseball wives. I was tired of all the bullshit. The only ray of hope was my sister Sam, who had moved again to San Francisco with her husband. That was the one thing that kept me from falling apart—the knowledge that at least I'd have one true friend in California.

Jose went off for spring training in late February, and—in the interest of self-preservation—Josie and I went with him. But one night he came back to the hotel and looked upset.

"What's wrong?" I asked.

"None of the other wives are here," he said. "Why do you have to be here? Don't you think you and Josie would be happier at home?" My jaw literally dropped, and I found myself in tears. "What's the big deal?" Jose asked. "You can come back in a couple of weeks."

The bastard. He was tired of having his wife and daughter around. He was ready for some serious fun.

I took Josie and went home to Weston, and the following morning I woke up to find a message on my cell phone. "Listen, you don't know me," the woman said. "But five minutes after you left, I was with Jose in his room." She went on to describe some of the baby things I'd inadvertently left behind, as if I needed proof. I thought she was being unnecessarily cruel, but the message continued. "I just feel real bad about what I did. When I saw that baby stuff and everything, it kind of hit me. I wanted you to know I was sorry and that it won't happen again. You can call me if you want to ask me anything."

Maybe Jose had treated her badly. I don't know. I didn't want to know. I didn't call. And I never said a word about it to Jose. What was the point?

When the time came, I flew to Oakland. We got a house in a nice area called Blackhawk about half an hour away from the stadium. Jose liked it there. He had lived in Blackhawk years earlier with Esther, during a long-ago season with the Oakland Athletics, the team that had launched his career.

Jose wanted Vera to come, but I said no. "I want to raise my own daughter." I said.

"It's a mistake. You can't do this yourself."

"I can, and I will," I said.

It was hell. I was trying to keep Josie on a schedule. I was trying to keep the house nice. I was trying to cook and clean for my husband. I became a pretty good cook that season, and Jose loved it.

I was the perfect wife. From time to time, I'd take Josie to a game with me, and I'd cheer from the stands. The other perfect wives came over and cooed at my little baby, and they all went out of their way to tell me how wonderful I looked. They thought I was glowing with happiness. I wish I could have talked to them. I wish I could have told them that Jose hadn't said more than ten words to me that season. I think the longest sentence I'd heard from him came one night after a pasta dinner, angel hair in Alexander sauce, a pink sauce with vodka, scallops, shrimp, and a little whitefish. "That's my favorite dish," he said, before leaving the table to call one of his little girlfriends.

And there *were* girlfriends. Believe me. I could smell them on him. I was doing my best to make a happy home for him, to be the perfect wife, but he didn't give a damn.

He didn't even want to go out. He went out every night when the team was on the road, and every night he had his needs met, sexual and otherwise. But when he was home, he wasn't interested. When he was home, he'd concentrate on resting for the next round of girls.

"Come on," I said. "Let's go to a nice restaurant and have a good time."

"I'm tired," he said.

I was tired, too, and I didn't really feel like going out, but I wanted to make him happy. I could be a triple threat—wife, mother, and slut.

When he was playing baseball, I'd take Josie with me to the local gym—they had a nursery—and decided to get into the best shape I could. I knew I looked good, but I wanted to look better. I wanted Jose to find me irresistible. Jose liked some meat on me, and I was adding inches to my physique to make him happy.

One evening, during a home game, I saw a familiar groupie in the stands, and at first I couldn't place her. But then I remembered: I had seen her in a number of old photographs that dated back to the Esther years. I had asked Jose about her, and in a rare moment of candor he admitted that he'd slept with her "once or twice," during a rocky period in his marriage. He was quick to point out, however, that she didn't mean a thing to him. None of them meant anything to him.

The groupie looked at me and quickly looked away. In my heart I just knew. I turned to the baseball wife on my left, pointed the girl out, and asked, "Do you know who that is?"

"No," she said, dutifully honoring the code. "I've never seen her before."

I went home, crushed. The next morning, I called Vera and asked her to come to Oakland to help me. I didn't have the energy for the marriage anymore. I was weak, tired, and very close to being defeated. Nothing was working out. I couldn't make Jose happy.

I went to see my sister, and I could see I was just depressing her, so I went back to the house and called my mother, but I just depressed her, too.

A few days later, with Jose away at a game in Texas, I went to have my hair done at the hot salon in town, thinking it would lift my spirits. One of the girls who worked there recognized me as Jose's wife. By sheer coincidence, she shared an apartment with the groupie I'd seen in the stands. And by sheer coincidence, Jose had left a message on their answering machine that very morning.

The girl at the salon liked me and felt sorry for me. She dialed her home number and punched in her code and let me hear the message. It was Jose, all right, and it had been a long time since I'd heard that much energy in his voice. "Get your sexy ass down to Texas, girl. I miss you, and I want to see you right now."

I was heartbroken. I handed the phone back to the girl, and I saw my reflection staring back at me. My eyes flooded with tears. When was I going to get the message? When was it going to be enough?

This was in July 1997, right before another back injury sidelined Jose for the rest of the season. I called him in Texas. "So I hear that little slut is on her way to Texas." I said.

"What are you talking about?" he asked.

"Fuck you, Jose. You're a lying sack of shit." This time I was emotionally prepared to handle the truth. I'd had plenty of evidence prior to this, on plenty of other occasions, but this time I was determined to handle it. This time I was finally going to do the right thing.

I got back to the house and told Vera I was leaving. "I can't take it anymore," I said. "It's not working out for Jose and me. He is not a good man. I thought he was going to change, but he's never going to change."

I asked her to help me pack, and two days later, the day he

was due back, I believe I crossed paths with him on the way to the airport.

"Where are you?" he asked. "Why aren't you here?"

"I'm at the airport, on my way to Miami," I replied. "And you know why I'm not there."

"Don't do this to us," he said.

"I didn't do this to us," I said. "You did. I've done nothing but try to be perfect for you, and it's not enough. I don't even exist. I get nothing from you."

"Jessica, I love you. Please come back."

I hung up. I'd heard that more than a few times, and if that was the best loving I was going to get from Jose, I could live without it.

The moment I landed in Miami, I called Jean Renard in Boston and told him I needed a good divorce attorney. "I'm sorry to hear that," he said, but he was just being polite. Jean had seen the futility of my staying with Jose long before I had.

"I'm still young," I told him. "I'm in the best shape of my life. And I have to think of my daughter."

Ironic, isn't it? At one point, Josie is what kept me in the marriage. Now Josie was giving me the strength to get out. I had to protect her from this. I was going to be happy, both for her sake and mine.

Jean put me in touch with an attorney in Boca Raton who had handled some big-name clients. I walked him through the whole sordid story. The cheating. The lies. The emotional abuse. The self-absorption. I even told him about the bacterial infections, which had been so numerous I'd lost count.

He asked me if I was sure I wanted to proceed, and I told him there was absolutely no doubt in my mind.

"We're going to serve Jose," he said. "He will have thirty days to respond."

I went home terrified. I was finally taking control of my life. But this time I meant it. This time I was determined to go through with it.

I reached Jose in Oakland that same afternoon. "Jose, I just went to see an attorney. I'm filing for divorce."

"What?! Don't do this to me! I love you. You're my wife. You and Josie are my family. Think about that!"

"That's exactly what I'm thinking about. Me and Josie. If *you* had thought about *us,* even a tiny bit, this wouldn't be happening."

Right on cue, Jose injured his back again. The season was over for him, and they were going to put him in rehab in Oakland, but he asked if he could go home for a little while. They let him go. He flew back to Florida and came home and tried to woo me back.

"There's nothing to talk about," I said, but I could already feel my resolve weakening. The addiction was kicking in again. I was staring at the whole Jose package—the way he looked, the familiarity, his eyes.

"We need to talk," he said.

"There's nothing to talk about, Jose."

"Look, I know I'm not perfect, but I love you, and I can do better."

It sounded like he had read an article in a men's magazine entitled "How to Get Your Girl Back After You Have Totally Fucked Up."

"I'm sick of it, Jose. I'm not doing this anymore."

He took me to bed. We made love. It was wonderful.

"Call off the dogs," he said.

"No," I said. "I don't want to stay married to you."

"Jessica, this is crazy. We can make this work."

"You've been saying that for four years."

I wasn't going to get sucked back in this time.

He kept getting calls from Oakland about coming back to do his rehab there, and he kept asking for more time, but they finally demanded that he get on a plane, and he packed his bags.

"Jessica, I love you. Please don't give up on us."

When he left, everything felt much easier. There was one moment of weakness when I called my lawyer and his team to tell them I might want to reconsider, but they quickly set my troubled mind at ease. I could tell from their reaction that they thought I should go through with it. They no doubt had dealt with many husbands like Jose in the past, and they knew that he was just as bad as the others, if not worse. He would never change. He was a horrible, lying cheat, and he would continue to be a horrible, lying cheat for the rest of his miserable life.

By the time Jose returned from Oakland, I had moved Josie and myself into the guest room. I couldn't move out because I didn't have the means to move out and because I was waiting for the legal machinery to kick into gear.

Jose had been served, and he was pissed. He went from begging me to stay to screaming, and I screamed right back. When we got tired of screaming, he'd get into one of his fancy cars and race off, and he wouldn't come back till the wee hours.

This became a pattern. He would drag his sorry ass out of bed in the early afternoon and come looking for me to apologize. I wouldn't listen, and before long we'd be screaming again, and I'd be throwing anything within arm's reach. It seemed like Vera spent part of each day sweeping up broken glass.

"Please stay," he'd beg.

"No," I'd say. "I'm leaving."

"What do you want me to do? Get on my knees?"

"It wouldn't help. It's too late for that."

Then he'd get mad and scream some more, and I'd turn around, reaching for something to throw. I was running out of things to throw.

"You don't give a shit about me!" he'd yell. "Everything I've given you, and you only think of yourself!"

"You're wrong! That's the problem! I love you too much. But now I *am* going to think about myself. I don't want to be with a man like you. I deserve better. I'm going to find someone who appreciates the real me!"

"Fuck you!"

"No, fuck you!"

It was over. It was finally over.

Or so I thought.

It's Over

Jose finally gave me enough money to find a new place, to furnish it, and to keep me going for a few months. He didn't do it out of the kindness of his heart, though. It was mandated by law.

I wanted Vera to come with me, but he refused to let her go. He didn't know how to boil water. He was useless without her.

I found a place in Coconut Grove. It was nice, but it was relatively tiny. There was something psychologically debilitating about going from a 20,000-square-foot mansion to a two-bedroom apartment. It felt as if my life had suddenly become smaller, and in fact it *had* become smaller—but only because I was getting rid of the things that weren't working. Still, I liked the apartment. It was mine. My bed. My decorations. My choices. My space.

The next item on my agenda was finding a nanny, and I interviewed a dozen women before I found one I felt I could trust with my baby. My life was moving forward.

Jose still couldn't believe this was happening, and right until the day I moved out he remained in disbelief. He wasn't there the day I moved out—he went golfing, saying he didn't want to be there to see it—but he came to Coconut Grove the following night.

"I'm here to see my daughter," he said. And of course he spent the night. It was easier than talking and fighting. We fucked. The sex was good.

In the morning, the old Jose was back. "If you come home, I won't date anymore. I won't even look at other women. But if you don't come home, I'm going to start dating tomorrow."

"What's that? A threat?

"I'm just telling you," he said.

"Fine. I'll date, too. I have a few friends of my own."

Two nights later, to rub it in my face, he called me from a bar. I could hear the music and the voices of happy women, a grating, miserable sound.

"So why are you calling? To show me you're making good on your threat?"

"I'm just calling to see how Josie's doing. And stop complaining. I wouldn't be out here if my wife hadn't filed for divorce."

"That's right, Jose. It's my fault. You had nothing to do with it. It was just a whim. I was unhappy for no reason, and this is how I punish you."

"Can we talk about this?"

"What's the point?"

"Come on. Let's go out. What are you doing tomorrow?"

I went. What can I say? I was weak. We decided to invite one of my girlfriends along, thinking that it might help take the edge off, and the early part of the evening was pleasant and full of promise. But a few drinks into it, I started getting upset. Girls kept cruising by to say hello to Jose, and it irked the hell out of me. I knew it wasn't his fault, and I tried not to blame him, but at one point I caught him smiling back at a particularly shapely young lady. It just killed me. I didn't want him rubbing it in my face.

"I'm leaving," I said. "I'm tired of this."

I got up and left, and my girlfriend followed me outside. I was a little tipsy, and felt I shouldn't drive, so I handed her my car keys and asked her to take me home. As we were beginning to pull away, Jose hurried out of the bar. She stopped, and he climbed into the back seat.

"Who's this guy Eddie I'm hearing about?" he asked abruptly. We were barely halfway down the block. Eddie lived down the street from my new place. He was just a nice, decent guy. Nothing was going on.

"He's a friend," I said, wondering who had told him about Eddie. "And why is it your business? You can have friends but I can't? Fuck you and your double standard."

Jose had been drinking more than usual, and suddenly he was in a very ugly mood. "You're hanging out with a bad crowd," he said. "I'm going to take Josie away from you."

"I don't want to talk about this, Jose. Not now, and not in front of my friend. And you're in no shape."

He ignored me. "I'm going to get custody of Josie. She's better off in my big house instead of that little place with all those creeps around. And I have family who cares about Josie. Your family's not even here."

"Oh yeah? Who came down to help me when she was born?"

"I'm going to take her away. I'm a good father."

"You're a lousy father. All you care about is you. And you were a lousy husband. That's why we are where we are today."

"Fuck you."

"You're crazy," I said. "All the steroids have finally made you totally crazy."

He punched me in the back of the head, and I whirled in my seat. "All right! That's it! I'm calling the cops." I whipped out my cell phone and dialed 911, and he kept haranguing me from the back seat. "Put that phone down! I hardly touched you, you bitch!"

By this time we were pulling into my apartment complex, and we got out of the car, still screaming and fighting. Jose began to move toward his Bentley, sick of the whole thing, and just then the police showed up. I was fuming, still screaming at Jose, "You're not going to hit me ever again, you bastard! How dare you threaten to take my daughter?!"

"What are you fucking talking about?" Jose asked. "I barely touched you!"

The police could see Jose had been drinking, and he's a big guy, so they weren't taking any chances. They made him turn around and cuffed him. I didn't give a shit. I felt good. The police said they'd take Jose down to the station in the cruiser, and they asked if I minded following in my own car, with my girlfriend, who had witnessed the whole thing. I said I didn't mind. I got back in and she followed them to the precinct.

"I'm sorry I got you into this," I told my girlfriend.

"You didn't get me into anything," she said. "Jose did."

When I found myself inside the police station, I suddenly began to feel less confident. It had been a short ride, but those few minutes had sobered me up a little.

"Are you afraid of him?" one of the cops asked me.

"Yes," I said. "A little."

"You think he would hurt you?"

"I don't know," I said. "He punched me in the back of the head in the car. And he threatened to take my daughter." I was feeling worse with every passing second. Part of it was the alcohol, but part of it was the fact that my life had been reduced to this.

"Where else did he hit you?"

"He didn't," I said, feeling even worse. It's not as if they were pressuring me, but they wanted to get the whole story, and they wanted me to go over every detail. I told them how long we'd been at the bar, how much we'd had to drink, and I described the incident that had set me off. Then I told them about Jose following me out and getting into the car, and I repeated every detail. As the story poured out of me, I felt increasingly lousy. I couldn't believe I was talking about my life. I deserved better than this, and so did Jose. "I think we'll be okay," I said. "We just had too much to drink and said some ugly things, but I think we'll be fine."

They decided to let him go, and as I walked out I saw him at the far end of the room, signing autographs for the cops. I left the precinct, got back in my car, and my friend drove me home. I don't know how Jose got back. Maybe they gave him a police escort.

The next day, the police followed up with a phone call, but I told them I didn't want to press charges. I told them again that I felt I had drank too much and that in the light of day the whole thing seemed as if it had been blown out of proportion. In the light of day I also wondered whether I'd been *looking* for a fight. I was mad at Jose, justifiably so, but I was also mad at myself for being there. I wondered whether I wanted to push him into the type of ugly confrontation from which there would be no return. If that had been my intention, I'd failed.

The only people who got anything out of the whole fiasco were members of the press, who somehow dug up the story and went to town with it. Jose had always maintained that the press didn't like him, and on this particular occasion I had to agree with him. The reporters went out of their way to make him look as bad as possible, and some of them even took the time to review every questionable incident in his past, dating back to the years he was with Esther. As a result of all of the attention, he was ordered to take anger management classes—despite the fact he hadn't been charged with anything. I felt bad for him, and I called to tell him so. He felt pretty lousy himself, and he came over to visit and be consoled, and we ended up spending the night together. In the morning, the photographers were outside my place, waiting for him. The next day, there were photographs of him in the paper, leaving my apartment. They were determined to make him out to be a wife beater. And to make it look as if I, the beaten wife, wasn't smart enough to make it stop.

My attorney was delighted. All of this worked in our favor, he explained. "He'll never get custody. He's abusive. He ran his first wife off the road at 125 miles an hour."

I didn't like the sound of this. Nobody really knew what had happened between Jose and Esther in that car accident, but somehow he was the bad guy. I was trying to take the moral high road, and I repeated what I had told the cops: that we'd been drinking; that Jose just lost control and whacked me on the back of the head; that I'd antagonized him at the bar, which made me part of the problem. But they didn't want to hear any of that. They told me to keep my distance. They didn't want to see me out with Jose. It wouldn't help my case.

A few days later, some friends took me to a football game in Miami. After the game, I met Tony Gonzalez, one of the Kansas City Chiefs. He was incredibly sweet. He also happens to be six-feet-five inches and 250 pounds of pure muscle, and—much as I hate to admit it—I was attracted to him. Or maybe I should put it another way—I was attracted to the idea that there was another man out there who would love me properly and that could actually be as gorgeous as Jose. Most women know exactly the type of men they are attracted to, and I'm no exception. I like my men tall, strong, and beautiful.

Tony and I exchanged numbers and spent hours talking on the phone. He was wonderful. I was in a very fragile place, admittedly, but he seemed genuine.

As for Jose, whenever he reached me on the phone, all he did was scream at me. He was sick of the lawyers, sick of fighting, and sick of not being able to fix things between us. I was sick of hearing what he was sick of, and our conversations always ended badly. In one sense, this was a good thing. I got to a place where I *knew* it was over. There was no way I was ever going to get back with Jose.

Then Tony called to invite me to come see him in Kansas

City. I decided to go. Jose had been bugging me to let him keep Josie for a few days, saying he wasn't seeing enough of her, and I thought this would be the perfect time to accommodate him. I drove up to Weston and left her with him, and we got through it without incident.

"I'm going to go up to Cleveland for a night," I lied.

"You look real good," he said.

"Thanks," I said, and I forced myself to walk away.

When I got back to Coconut Grove, I picked up the phone and booked a ticket on Delta, which was a mistake. Jose's best friend worked at Delta, and Jose wasn't buying my story about Cleveland, so he called the guy to check up on me. My cell phone began to ring the moment the plane landed in Kansas City. I just knew it was Jose, and I decided to not answer it. He was in panic mode. He wouldn't stop calling. I finally turned off the ringer and put the phone on vibrate. I was thinking, *Fuck you. This will make up for the two or three hundred girls you slept with while you were with me.* I thought back to when we first met, back in Ohio, so many years before, when I had asked him how many women he'd slept with. "Twelve or fifteen," he had told me. I guess he'd been talking about the previous *week.*

I liked Tony. I wouldn't have been going off to see him if I wasn't seriously attracted to him. But a part of me, the lesser part of me, also wanted to hurt Jose. I knew it was wrong, but I couldn't help myself. I wanted him to know what it felt like. I wanted him to know what I'd endured.

Tony picked me up at the airport. We went out for dinner and drinks, and he then took me to his place. My cell phone hadn't stopped ringing, so at one point I excused myself and finally picked it up. "Hello?"

"Jessica, it's me."

"I know," I said.

"Why haven't you been answering my calls?"

"I didn't know you were calling," I said.

"Where you at?"

"I told you. I'm home. Visiting my mother."

"No, you're not."

I guess I didn't really want to hurt him. Or, if I had wanted to hurt him, the feeling suddenly passed. I felt like shit now. "Yes, I am," I insisted quietly.

"Jessica, I know where you're at. Do you have something you want to tell me?"

"No. Nothing."

"You're in Kansas City with Tony Gonzalez."

At the time, I didn't know who had ratted me out, and I was a little thrown. But I didn't have the energy to deny it. "Okay. You're right. I'm here to see Tony."

Jose didn't say anything for a moment because he was crying. "I can't believe you," he said, choking up.

"I'm sorry, Jose. This isn't about you. We're not together anymore. I'm just trying to get on with my life."

"Did you sleep with him?"

"No. I just got here."

"Are you going to?"

"I can't talk about this, Jose."

Suddenly he was sobbing. It was the only time I had ever

heard Jose really cry, and it tore me up. I didn't know how to deal with it, and I didn't want to deal with it, so I hung up.

Tony and I made love that night. I needed to be held, and here was a guy who was decent and respectful and wanted to hold me.

Jose's night turned out to be a lot less pleasant. If you believe what he wrote about the incident in his book, *Juiced,* a title that inspired this book's title, he almost killed himself that night. "There's no description for that kind of pain," he wrote. "It hits you all at once and overwhelms you. It feels impossible that one man could endure that much pain."

Really, Jose? What about women? Are we incapable of feeling pain?

He wrote that he was already depressed about his career and that he was tired of being depicted by the media as an outsider, an outlaw, and a villain. At that point, the story got pretty dramatic—Jose was so depressed about Tony and me that he went and got his gun, something he called a "street sweeper." He was just about to put himself out of his misery when "something very strange happened."

"From somewhere indistinct nearby, I heard my daughter make a kind of strange sound, a little squeal, a quiet cry."

Jose put the gun down and went to see his little girl, and he decided he would go on living. That's his story, anyway. He never shared it with me. The first time I learned about it was when I read it in his book.

Meanwhile, back in Kansas City, Tony and I got up and went out for breakfast. Then he drove me to the airport and made his way to the stadium. It had been a pleasant visit, and it was never going to turn into anything else. Neither of us expected more, and neither of us wanted more.

When I got back to Miami, I went up to Weston to get Josie, and I made sure Jose wasn't around. On my way back to Coconut Grove, Tony reached me on my cell. "Jose called," he said.

"Oh?"

"I'm not going to get into detail, but I don't want to be in the middle of this. I'm not looking to be part of some O. J. Simpson thing."

"He was just upset. Don't worry. Nothing's going to happen."

"Take care of yourself," he said.

"I will," I said.

Jose called me later. "You really hurt me," he said.

"I don't want to talk about it," I said. I sounded just like him.

"I can't believe you did that to me," he said and hung up.

In the weeks ahead, I tried to get on with my new life in Miami. I had met several people in my apartment complex; they seemed nice enough, and I began to hang out with them. I had a nanny living with me, so it was manageable, but I always put Josie to bed myself. I wanted her to know who her mother was.

Once again, however, somebody ratted me out—maybe Jose had another private investigator following me. Jose called to say he didn't approve of the company I was keeping. "Those people are not nice people. You're looking for trouble." It was the same old song—he never liked anyone I liked. If I'd been having lunch with Mother Teresa, he would have found a flaw in her.

"I didn't approve of the company *you* kept when we were together," I said. "And we're not together now. So please keep your opinions to yourself."

The following week, a really nice young woman moved into a vacant unit down the hall from mine. She was twenty-four, single, and before long she was part of our little clique. I really liked her. I felt I could tell her anything, and I did.

In January 1998, I took a weekend trip to Jamaica with my new neighbor and other members of our clique. It was a fun, relaxing vacation, and it didn't involve any sex (for me, anyway). In fact, with the exception of a couple of hits of Ecstasy, there was no questionable behavior at all.

When we got back to Miami, I found out that my friendly neighbor was actually a private investigator. Jose had put her up in the unit down the hall and had paid her to keep an eye on me and my friends. She had culled profiles on each one of them, and it turned out that a few of them had run-ins with the law in the past. I was livid. I was also worried. I wondered if his lawyers had put him up to it. Maybe they were looking for ways to attack me and show I was a bad mother.

"What did you get for your hundred thousand dollars, Jose? What did you find out? That I didn't sleep with anyone? That I'm not like you?"

"You took drugs!"

"Oh big deal! I took a little Ecstasy!"

"It wasn't even X!" he said. "I had it analyzed at the lab. It was speed!"

I didn't say anything, but suddenly I understood why I'd

been up all night cleaning. That hit of so-called Ecstacy had been a lot different from the hit I'd shared with Lorraine.

"I don't like those people," Jose droned on. "I told you already. Those people are going to get you into trouble. I'm looking out for you, and I'm looking out for my daughter. I'm not going to have my daughter hanging around with scumbags."

Not everyone in the clique was squeaky clean, true—one of them was actually busted a few months later, for money laundering—but they weren't as bad as Jose was making them out to be. What's more, I had never exposed my daughter to them. That was my own little world, a place I escaped to from time to time when life threatened to overwhelm me.

During one of those evenings out, a week or two after discovering the private investigator, I was introduced to a guy named Ira. He was single and had a baby out of wedlock with a now former girlfriend, but he was determined to be a good father. As we talked about our children, we bonded immediately. I found Ira to be as sweet and honest as they come, and we were soon dating.

Ira wanted to know everything about me, down to what life had been like on the farm in Ohio. I spoke to him about my childhood, my Olympic dreams, my stint as a ballerina, and even about my attempt at a college education. He was everything Jose wasn't—kind, attentive, considerate, and loving. But he wasn't Jose. As I got more deeply involved with him, I discovered, none too happily, that I was still pining for Jose. I didn't understand it, but I came to understand it later. I was really falling for the guy, so I actually began to see myself breaking free from Jose; that was the problem: I wasn't sure I was ready to let go.

On February 4, 1998, Jose signed as a free agent with the Toronto Blue Jays for $2.125 million. He called from time to time to check on Josie and tell me that he wished we were still together. "You're my family. Why can't we be a family again?"

Every time he called, I felt sad, and the sadness lingered. I missed some of what we had once had, and I missed what we could have had if Jose had been half the man I had imagined him to be. I was also troubled by how unhappy he sounded. There was genuine sorrow there. When he said he missed me and Josie, he really meant it. You couldn't fake the kind of emotion I was hearing.

I also knew that his sadness wasn't related to baseball. He was having a great season with Toronto. He was strong, his body seemed to be holding up, and he wasn't missing any games.

"I'm dating someone," I admitted.

"Who?" For once, he didn't fly off the handle.

"Just a guy. No one you know."

"What does he do?"

"Real estate. Car dealerships. Stuff like that."

"Do you love him?" Jose asked. "Does he make you happy?"

"I don't know," I said, and in a moment of weakness I added four little words that I should have kept to myself: "I still miss you."

"Please come back," Jose said.

I didn't know what to do. I told him I'd think about it—and I did—but I was seriously conflicted. I didn't know whether Jose could change. Do people ever change?

Ira seemed to be a good man for me, but I guess I was attracted to dysfunctional men.

A few days after that conversation, by pure coincidence, I met

Esther, Jose's first ex-wife, for the first time. She knew someone in the apartment complex, and they knew about me, so one afternoon the guy brought her by and introduced us. It was a little awkward at first—I could see her checking me out, and I checked her out right back—but I invited her in for a moment.

"You've done a really nice job on the place," she said.

She then met Josie, and she was bowled over by how pretty she was. She hadn't brought her own daughter, but she showed me pictures, and I thought she was very cute, too.

I couldn't believe I was finally meeting the famous Esther. She was certainly very beautiful, and she seemed so much more glamorous and sophisticated than me; but I took solace in the fact that she was also ten years older than me. Before she left, she gave me her phone number. "Call me some time," she said. "We'll have a drink."

After she left, I remember being struck by the fact that Esther wasn't the monster I had expected. I wasn't going to pass judgment based on our brief meeting, of course, but I got a nice feeling from her, and I trusted the feeling. I also felt bad for her. She and I had probably gone through very similar experiences with Jose. We were like two people who survived the same horrible accident. A gorgeous accident, an irresistible accident, but an accident nonetheless.

At one point, as she began to walk away, I had to fight the urge to run after her and ask her if she still loved Jose. Instead, I asked myself the question. The answer was no. I was free of him.

I plunged back into my relationship with Ira, trying to make it work, and I even helped him look for a new house. He was working on getting shared custody of his child, and he wanted a kid-friendly home.

One night, after another evening out with Ira, I returned to the apartment just as the nanny was getting ready to put Josie to bed. When I took her in my arms, hoping to put her to bed myself, she began to cry and reached for the nanny. The nanny took over, and Josie immediately quieted down. It killed me. I'm sure plenty of mothers have had similar experiences, regardless of their devotion to their children, but somehow it really floored me. I felt like I was failing my daughter. I was spending too much time with Ira and the gang. I was a selfish, lousy mother.

I cried myself to sleep that night. The nanny tried to comfort me, telling me it was normal, that she'd seen the same thing happen in many other homes with plenty of other kids, but it didn't register because I didn't want it to register. Much as I hate to admit it, and much as I dislike myself for it, I think I was looking for a reason to get back with Jose. And that was all the reason I needed. This single mother thing wasn't working for me. I wanted to be a better mother, and I wanted Josie to grow up with her real dad.

I called Jose the next day. "Let's try to make this work," I said.

He was overjoyed. "I'm so happy. I was so depressed about all of this. Thank you for coming back to me."

I called my attorneys and told them I didn't want to go through with the divorce, and they urged me to carefully think this through. "This is a very emotional time for you, Jessica," one of them told me. "Are you sure you're thinking clearly? Are you sure you want to stay married to this man?"

"I'm sure," I said. "I know what I want."

Then I called Ira. We met for dinner. I told him I was going to try to make things work with Jose.

"I had a feeling this was going to happen," he said.

"There's a very powerful bond there," I explained. "We're a family. I want to try again. I feel like I'm letting this defeat me."

Ira didn't judge me. He was disappointed, but he was also understanding.

As for Jose, he sounded happier every time we spoke on the phone. He was all the way up in Toronto, but he arranged to have someone come to the apartment, help me pack my things, and take them up to the house in Weston.

Josie and I didn't even go to Weston. We went to the airport and flew directly to Toronto, and Jose picked us up. He was beaming. He looked like a changed man. He took us back to the place he'd rented for the season, where Vera was waiting for us. She was also excited to have us back.

In the days ahead, we began to settle in. It was a little awkward at first—we'd been apart for almost one year—and I found myself struggling to readjust to the whole wife role. But it was good to be back.

"Mr. Canseco was very sad while you were away," Vera confided. "He hardly ever went out. All he thought about was you and little Josie." If that was true, that was a good thing. Maybe we were finally getting through to him.

Still, it wasn't easy. I missed my friends in Miami, I missed my independence, and there were times when I wondered if this had all been a big mistake. On some days, Jose was as quiet and as uncommunicative as ever, and I missed Ira. On others, he seemed worried about me. "You're too skinny. You look pale. Let's get you eating better. You don't have to be stressed anymore. Everything's going to be fine." I liked that Jose a lot better.

Before long, I got back into the swing of being married and into the life of a baseball wife. Jose was having a good season. He would end it with 46 homers, 107 RBIs, and 29 stolen bases, and he played in more than 150 games—something he hadn't managed to do in years. It was his best season since 1991—not that he was getting much attention. This was 1998, the year that his old Oakland teammate Mark McGwire and Sammy Sosa shattered Roger Maris's single season home-run record, which had been considered unbreakable. McGwire got there first, as everyone now knows, in a game against Sosa and the Cubs, and the entire country was captivated by the two players.

Jose was equally captivated, if for other reasons. "Look how big those guys are," he said. "Looks like everyone is getting on the bandwagon."

He meant steroids, of course. As far as he was concerned, half the players were getting juiced. And he was fine with it. What he objected to was the fact that they denied it—that they behaved as if they had earned all that power and muscle on their own in the gym. Many players were getting juiced. He had been juiced for years, and in his book he wrote that getting juiced is the future of professional sports. I didn't know whether it was the future, but I was there for Jose in the old familiar role of Nurse Jessica.

I wanted more than that, though. If I'd learned anything from my time apart from Jose, it was that I shouldn't rely on him to make me happy. It wasn't enough to be Mrs. Jose Canseco. I had to be my own person, and I had to learn to stand on my own two feet. I don't know exactly how I'd stumbled across that less-than-original notion—maybe I'd been reading too many cheesy articles in too many women's magazines—but, original or not, the idea made perfect sense. I didn't want to be the dependent little wife. If our marriage was going to work, I had to go to work on myself, and going to work on myself meant becoming responsible for my own happiness.

On more than one occasion, I had broached the subject with my mother, and she told me that it had taken her many years to learn that same lesson. She had depended on my father for absolutely everything and had waited until middle-age to get a life of her own. I was still young. I didn't have to make the same mistake.

Without telling Jose, I looked into the nursing program at Florida International University in Miami. As soon as I'd mapped out a schedule that looked as if it would work for me, I broke the news to him.

"A nurse?" he asked. "Why do you want to be a nurse?"

"You're going to need me to take care of you some day," I joked. I was only half-joking, actually. Jose may have had a good season, but the steroids were beginning to take their toll. There was always something wrong: back, hamstring, elbow, groin, neck. He knew it, and baseball knew it. The multiyear, multimillion dollar contracts were history. At this point in his career, he had to perform to collect those bonuses. And performing was getting tougher and tougher.

"I don't get it," he said, working hard at avoiding an argument. "This program's in Miami?"

"Yes," I said. At FIU. It starts in September."

"You're going to leave me again?"

"I'm not leaving you, Jose. I'm going to get an education. It'll be good for all of us."

He didn't see how it would be good for him, but he finally, grumblingly, relented.

At the end of August, I took Josie and flew to Miami. The night before I was supposed to enroll, the phone rang. It was almost 11:00 P.M. I assumed it was Jose, but I was wrong. It was my mother, and she was in a terrible panic: "Dad's not breathing!" she screamed. "He's on the couch, and he's not breathing!"

"Oh my God! What happened? Did you call 911?!"

"I called them! They're not here yet. He had a pain in his leg! He collapsed. I think he's dying!"

"Mom!" I said, equally panicked. "Pull yourself together!"

"Oh my God! The ambulance is here! I'll call you back."

She didn't call back, so I called her—and called and called. I didn't hear from her till four in the morning. In a very small, tired voice, she told me that he had passed away. He'd had an aneurysm, and the doctors had been unable to revive him. I began to weep quietly. My mom sounded lost and alone and utterly helpless. She and my father had been married for thirty-three years. It had been a terrible marriage, but she had relied on him for a lot, and—in his own, absent way—he had provided.

I knew she was lost without him.

"I'll be on the first available plane," I said.

I called Jose, packed a suitcase, grabbed Josie, and drove to the Miami airport, and we caught the next flight to Cleveland. When we arrived at the old farmhouse, it was even worse than anything I'd imagined. My mother was sitting there, wringing her hands, her eyes red and puffy. "What do I do now?" she asked. "What do I do with this house? How do I make decisions? What do I do with his car? What do I do with the truck? I don't know anything about his business. I don't know where to begin."

Jose couldn't come to Cleveland, but he was very supportive. He sent flowers and never stopped calling. Samantha and Rachel arrived that same day. We helped mom plan a little service at the house and arranged to have my father cremated. Samantha was the most grounded, and she pretty much took control of everything. We tried to adjust to the idea of my father's death, but we were all in a haze, sitting around like accident victims.

After the service, there was a short wake, and people slowly drifted back to their own lives. Then it was just the four of us again: Mom and her three daughters.

The next morning, while I was having breakfast, Samantha walked in and said she had to talk to me. She'd been out by the garage and looked a little pale.

"What's wrong?" I asked.

"Not here," she said. She took me aside, where she was sure no one could hear us. "I found some stuff under the front seat of Dad's truck," she said. She made a face that was part disgust and part confusion.

"He was cheating on mom?" I whispered.

"Worse," she said.

"What do you mean?" I asked.

"I'm going to show you," she said, leading me toward the front door. "But you can't tell mom."

11

CHAPTER

Family Secrets

My father was a cross-dresser—and more. My sister had found a folder beneath the seat of his truck. It was filled with letters and incriminating pictures, along with the keys to a storage locker. When we opened the storage locker, we were too stunned to speak. There were photographs of him dressed as a woman, and other photographs of him as a man, but not any version of a man we'd ever known about. He was half-naked and being whipped by a female flagellant.

There was more. He had many other folders corresponding to his various lives. There were classified ads ripped from newspapers: *Men Seeking Men.* There were copies of letters he had written to his male lovers, full of tender endearments, and there were letters from his lovers to him. There were even letters to and from a dominatrix, in which she wrote that he was overdue for another whipping.

I glanced at one of the letters. "I am torn between you and my family," he had written to a male lover in San Francisco. I didn't want to see more.

There were items in the storage locker that were almost too disturbing to think about. Handcuffs. Dildos. Some strange device that seemed designed to administer electric shocks to the nipples. Or worse.

It was horrifying and illuminating at the same time. We began to understand why my father was never home, why he'd chosen to put his family in a farmhouse far from his secret life in the city, and why he was so uninterested in his wife and his three little girls. I remembered how he used to shave off his mustache at regular intervals, then just as suddenly grow it back again. He had seemed like two distinct people to me when he did this, even then, as a child, and I saw that in many ways that's exactly what he was: two distinct people.

My sister and I sat in the storage unit, sifting through the evidence, reading the letters, one more horrifying and incriminating than the next, and we found ourselves in tears. How could we not tell mom? But how could we break it to her?

I felt horrible for her. She had spent the better part of her life trying to figure out why she couldn't get through to that remote, absent, disconnected man, and this went a long way toward explaining it. He was only a husband in name, just as he was only a father by default—he had a bizarre secret life that provided the thrills he didn't get at home.

When Samantha and I had seen enough, we decided we had to tell mom, and we went back to the house, sat her down on the living room couch, and broke the news to her as gently as possible. We had brought along some of the letters, realizing that they would tell the story better than we could, and we watched as she read them. Her eyes filled with tears, and she shook her head from side to side, not wanting to believe it. But when she finally pulled herself together, bits and pieces of the larger puzzle began to fall into place.

"I have to tell you girls a few things about your father," she said, still dabbing at her eyes. "I knew he wasn't well. Many years ago, ten or fifteen years ago, I found a catalog for women's clothes among his things. I asked him about it, and he said it had come in the mail, and he had been curious enough to flip through it. But it's almost as if he wanted to tell me because he went on to say that for a brief period as a boy he had enjoyed dressing up in women's clothes."

"Did you ask him for details?"

"Yes. He told me he wasn't doing it anymore, and I wasn't sure I believed him, so I went to see an attorney about getting a divorce. Your father begged me not to leave him, and he convinced me that it had all taken place in the distant past." She then indicated the few letters we had shared with her, and made a vague, sweeping gesture with her hand, as if they were unimportant. "All of this was a very long time ago." She said.

"*Mom,*" Samantha said, reaching for one of the letters. "This was written less than a year ago. 'I am torn between you and my family.'"

She shook her head, not wanting to believe it. The proof of his double life was staring her in the face, but it was easier to avert her eyes. I guess we really do believe what we want to believe.

Later in the day, I called Jose and told him all about it. He was as horrified as we were. "Your Dad? No way! It's not possible. He was such a quiet, normal guy. He seemed so conservative."

"None of us had a clue."

"I feel bad for your mother. How's she handling it?"

"Not well. She's in denial. Or maybe it's not sinking in."

It occurred to me that sometimes denial is all we have. Denial gets us from one day to the next. It didn't occur to me that I myself was in denial about my own life, and about my own husband, mostly because I was completely focused on my mother and her needs, but it would start becoming somewhat more clear in the days ahead.

"Is there anything I can do?" Jose asked me.

"No," I said. "Thanks. My sisters are all here, helping out. We'll take care of her."

During the trip back to Miami with Josie, I couldn't stop thinking about my father. I realized I had never told him I loved him, and I wondered whether that may have changed anything. He had never told me he loved me either, but in my troubled mind that wasn't the issue. I felt somehow responsible for his strange double life, as if perhaps I had driven him away. I wanted to apologize for not being a perfect daughter, for not being a perfect student, for having borrowed his car without permission. It was my fault that he wasn't happy. And if he didn't love me, that was my fault, too.

When I returned, Jose was a perfect prince for the first few days, but then he went back to being his old self. I had been obsessively thinking about my father and I had been worrying about my mother just as obsessively, but now I began to steal a moment here and there to think about myself. I began to wonder about the similarities between Jose and my father, absent men who came and went as they pleased, showed little emotion, and were hopelessly self-absorbed. Jose's life was less secret, and his behavior probably couldn't be described as aberrant, but his attitude toward me was as damaging as my father's attitude had been to my mother. There was a level of abuse in both cases, and in both cases we women endured it with minimal protest. I began to wonder why I couldn't stand up for myself, and why I kept going back for more abuse. I suspected I was turning into my mother.

Then again, I had learned by example. *You don't leave a marriage. You live with your decision, no matter how unhappy you may be.* She had done it. And I was doing it now. To walk away would have been an admission of defeat.

Somehow, for many reasons, my father's death began to change everything. It made me think about the lies people tell themselves, and tell one another, simply to keep going. I wanted to stop lying to myself, but I didn't know where to start.

On September 19, 1998, Alex Rodriguez joined the forty-forty club. Jose didn't say anything about it, and I didn't ask him. It was probably subconscious: I wanted to be less interested in him; I wanted to begin to break free again.

Jose came home at the end of the season, and in December he signed as a free agent with the Tampa Bay Devil Rays. Even after a terrific season, he couldn't get the big contract he was looking for, and he was not happy about it.

I didn't want to deal with his unhappiness, so I focused on doing something about my own misery. I had missed out on nursing school because of my father's death, but I was still determined to get an education. In one of my magazines, I had read about the

Florida College of Natural Health. They had a program for something called a paramedical esthetician. It was in the skin care field, but at a much higher level than the services offered at a local salon. It sounded interesting to me. There was a 600-hour program, and a 1,200-hour program, and the latter sounded like it had more potential. I sent away for more information.

I invited Mom down for Christmas. She was glad for the company, but it was not exactly a festive time. I was happy to have my mom there, but Jose was gloomy, and his moods affected us both. The days ran into one another with a tired sameness. We sat in the shade and played with Josie. I saved the turtle from yet another tumble into the pool. I snarled at the iguanas if they came too close.

When I talked to my mother, I found myself complaining incessantly about Jose, as she had once complained to me about Dad. I was like a broken record, and I began to hate the sound of my own voice. I realized I had to do something about it.

"We need to get into counseling," I told Jose after my mother had returned to Cleveland.

"Why? What's wrong?"

"Everything's wrong. You're not happy, and I'm not happy. The marriage isn't working."

Initially, he refused to go, but eventually I resorted to crying and begging, and he decided to give it a try. We went to see a woman, and Jose hardly talked at all. He sat there like a big lump, looking bored. I talked about my childhood, my parents' marriage, and my fear that I couldn't make Jose happy. And I talked about the way Jose belittled me and my needs, sometimes deliberately, and sometimes through sheer neglect.

"I'm sorry you feel that way, honey," Jose said, but he said it with a sarcastic edge, and it was obvious that he didn't mean it. He was belittling me again. He had learned this behavior from his father, just as I had learned to put up with his bad behavior from my mother.

The therapist wanted us to talk to each other about our feelings, and to work on the relationship ourselves, but Jose was looking for concrete answers, and a quick fix, so he dismissed her as useless. He didn't like all this talk about *feelings*. He thought that only made things worse.

In some ways, strangely enough, he was right. I began to sound like a therapist. "Just because your dad put you down, doesn't mean you have to do the same to me . . .

"Have you ever wondered whether your need to sleep with so many women is connected to your feelings of worthlessness? . . .

"Why do you have to control me?

"What are you worried about?

"Did your mother's death create abandonment issues for you?"

It was insane. And it was made worse by the fact that Jose was off the steroids again and slowly but surely slipping back into that dark, dismal, sexless place.

"Leave me alone with all that psychobabble!" he said. "I don't want to talk about it."

"You never want to talk about anything."

"You're right. I don't. So let's drop it."

Day by day, I felt him slipping away, and it made me furious. He was just as pissed, but he controlled himself. He'd already been through one round of anger management classes, not to mention several weeks' worth of bad press, and he was in no mood to go through that again. Still, who knew if they would have paid attention? He wasn't the same Jose Canseco anymore. The bad boy of baseball wasn't as newsworthy as he'd once been.

Finally, I became as removed and distant with Jose as he was with me. We were two strangers who happened to be living under the same roof with our young daughter, but we had absolutely nothing else in common. Our life was a total fucking bore, and we both knew it, and before long we decided to break the monotony by going out. If nothing else, there'd be other people around, something to look at besides each other. The liquor helped too. Alcohol always eased the pain.

There was one little problem, however. We would inevitably run into the few friends I had made in Miami when we went out. They would come over and say hello, and Jose wouldn't even look at them. The moment they were out of earshot he'd tell me that they were horrible and disgusting and that he couldn't understand how I'd allowed myself to hang around with that type of scum. As a result, our efforts at distraction only made things worse. Jose and I would be sitting at one end of the club, not talking, and my *horrible, disgusting, scummy* friends would be at the other end. I would have much rather been with them, but that wasn't going to happen. Jose hated everyone. No one was good enough for Jose.

"What are you always so angry about?" I asked.

"Those people were bad for you."

One night, Ira showed up, and he came by to say hello. He was a perfect gentleman and showed nothing but the utmost respect for both Jose and me, before going on his way. Jose was livid. It was something of a miracle that he hadn't ripped off the guy's head. It wasn't so much that he disliked Ira, however; it was more that Ira reminded him of our time apart. That upset him horribly, which made me realize I'd been right about his abandonment issues. The idea of being left alone absolutely killed him.

"I'm not going anywhere," I told him one night. I should have been going somewhere, but I remained trapped in the role of the dutiful wife, endlessly ministering to her man. I was definitely *thinking* of going somewhere, however, because I'd applied to and been accepted by the Florida College of Natural Health. The final hurdle involved breaking the news to Jose, but I wasn't ready to deal with that. So I continued to reassure him: "I'm here, aren't I? I hardly ever leave the house without you. What are you so worried about?"

Somehow, the words made an impression. Or seemed to, anyway. One night in February, we ran into Ira again, with his new girlfriend, Rhonda, and they asked us to join them at their table. Surprisingly enough, Jose was okay with it. It helped that Ira had moved on; it told Jose that he was over me. Jose didn't say much, of course. He never said much, but the fact that he was even sitting there was a giant step in the right direction. We had a couple of drinks, and I made pleasant conversation with Ira and Rhonda, and after a while Jose said it was time to leave.

When we got outside, it immediately became apparent that it

had been a huge struggle for him to keep his emotions in check. "I can't fucking believe you made me sit with those trashy people!" he bellowed.

"What are you talking about?! They're not trashy!"

"You fucked that guy!"

"Jose, that's over! It was over a long time ago!"

"Those disgusting fucking people," he said, and he was shouting all the way to the car. "Everyone in that world fucks everyone else."

"That's not true! And stop being so judgmental! You don't know anything about any of those people."

"They're probably all drug addicts!"

"No they're not. And what about you? You take drugs."

"Steroids aren't drugs!" he protested. "I'm doing it for my career! *I'm doing it for us!*"

"Keep doing them!" I said. *"They're going to fucking kill you!"*

"Oh you'd like that, wouldn't you?!"

It was two o'clock on a Saturday morning, and we were getting into Jose's Bentley, screaming at the tops of our lungs, unable to stop ourselves. Jose started telling me that I was a lousy wife and a worse mother and that last little barb really set me off. I backhanded him, and my watch caught on his lip. He then backhanded me and hit my eye.

I got out of the car, stunned, and I remember standing there, dazed, just as Scott Erickson, the Baltimore Orioles pitcher, sauntered past. "Are you okay?" he asked.

"Yes," I said, but I wasn't okay. I was sobbing.

"You sure?"

"Yes," I repeated. "I'm fine!"

Jose was still screaming at me.

"Jessica! Get back in the fucking car!"

I looked over at him. His lip was gushing blood onto his shirt.

"Get back in the fucking car right fucking now!" he screamed.

I got back in the car and shut the door. He pulled out, the tires screeching, and we drove home in total silence.

Two days later, we put Josie in the Mercedes-Benz and drove to Tampa for spring training. In a pathetic sort of way, it was kind of funny. He had a fat lip, and I had a black eye.

We didn't talk for several days. We were out at dinner one night, just him, me, and little Josie, and I broke the news about school. He was *very* supportive. "If you leave here, we're done," he snarled.

"Why does it have to be that way, Jose?" I said, fighting the urge to cry.

"Because I want you here."

"They don't have a program like that in Tampa. I looked into it, believe me."

"Find another program."

"I can't," I said. "That's the one I'm interested in. It really appeals to me. I think I'd be good at it. I'd be working with doctors to help people."

"What are you going to do with Josie?" he asked, and for a moment I hoped he was about to change his mind and let me go off to school.

"I've already thought of that," I said. "I'm putting her in day care."

"You leave, we're finished."

I refused to cry, and I didn't want to fight anymore, so I screamed at myself in my own head: *Why are you with this bastard?! What is wrong with you?! This has nothing to do with love! You're sick! When are you going to break free from him?!* Then I said, "Please don't give me an ultimatum, Jose. This is important to me."

"The relationship is important to me!"

"Is it?" I asked. "I haven't seen any changes."

"I have," he said, barely controlled. "You fucked a couple of other guys!"

Jesus. He was going to throw that in my face.

"We weren't together at the time, remember?"

"That's right. And if you leave, we won't be together ever again."

That was the end of the conversation. He paid for dinner, we went back to the house, and I put Josie to bed. By the time I got back to the bedroom, Jose was asleep and snoring. It was louder than ever. "Get off the steroids, you fat bloated fuck!" I muttered under my breath. "The steroids aren't killing you, but they make you snore." He snorted once or twice, like a porker, and went back to sleep.

In the morning, after he'd left for practice, I packed up, grabbed my little girl, and left. I was going to go to school. It was important to me. I felt scared but empowered.

Jose called that day and was not as angry as I had expected him to be. Maybe he was having a hard time believing that I'd actually taken off. "I told you, Jose. I really need to do this. It will be good for both of us. I'd like to have a career, too. It's not much fun being a baseball wife. I want a life of my own. I need some mental stimulation."

He called again the next day, and the day after that, and when he saw that I wasn't going to change my mind, he resorted to the old threats. "If you don't come back, I'm filing for divorce."

"Jose, stop that. I can't just follow you around for the rest of my life. I want to be a good wife and a good mom, but I also want to do something meaningful. I want a legitimate career. I'm tired of shopping. I'm tired of hanging out by the pool."

"You heard me. You come back, or I file for divorce."

"Why can't you meet me halfway? Why does it have to be all or nothing? This will make me a better, stronger person. Don't you want that for me?"

"Fuck you," he said. "Come back, or we're finished."

On April 14, 1999, Jose hit his 400th home run. Twenty-seven players had done it before him, but he was the first one who'd been born outside of the United States.

As I started getting ready for school, Jose made good on his promise. The doorbell rang one afternoon and a guy handed me divorce papers. I called my attorneys, and although they were supportive, I couldn't help feeling that inside they were gloating. I could almost hear them saying, *We told you to go through with it. Didn't we warn you? Didn't we tell you to get divorced and get it over with? Didn't we say he'd never change?*

I had thirty days to respond. Jose knew this. He called me and spelled it out: "You can stop this real easy. All you have to do is come back to me."

"I want to go to school."

"You can go to school in Tampa."

"I can't. I told you, but you never listen. They don't have programs like that in Tampa, not on a schedule that works for me and Josie. This is what I want to do."

"You're going to sacrifice your family for this stupid skin doctor shit?"

"No. You're sacrificing the family because you can't meet me halfway."

"Fuck you. We're finished."

I moved out. I found an apartment in South Beach, took Josie with me, and hired a nanny to help me out. I went to school, and I was very happy. Jose and I hardly talked. The divorce proceeded. We made tentative custody arrangements and, once a month, for a few days at a time, I made sure Josie went to stay with her father.

Jose tended to get emotional when he had Josie, and on those occasions he would break down and call. "Please come back," he'd say. "I want my family back."

But I'd made up my mind. I was doing well in school, Josie was happy, and my life was balanced. I was focused on my daughter, on studying, and on my future, which was suddenly beginning to look quite promising. And when I did go out, I was always home at a reasonable hour.

My mom came to visit, and she was very impressed. "I can't believe it," she said. "You seem happier now. I'm glad you're in school. Your life seems to be working out."

She was right. Things *were* working out. And I *was* happy. I had everything I needed. School, a home, a daughter. Well, not everything maybe. I didn't have a man, and I needed to be loved a little, as we all do. I met a number of decent guys, but none of them really did it for me. I know this is a terrible thing to say, but none of them compared with Jose. He still exerted a tremendous pull over me. I wasn't free of him yet.

Jose continued to call, sensing my weakness, and I resisted.

Whenever Josie was with Jose, I would call Vera to check up on her. Strangely enough, she began to tell me about the various women Jose was seeing. At first I didn't understand it—I wondered whether she was trying to hurt me—but then I realized she was doing it to keep me from hurting myself. She liked me, and she'd been around long enough to understand the addictive nature of my relationship with Mr. Canseco, and she must have known I was still hooked. "I think it's wonderful you're in school," she said. "I'm proud of you and happy for you."

One evening, still struggling with my feelings, I called Esther. "I'm sorry to bother you," I said. "I need to talk to you."

"No bother at all," she said.

Esther probably knew Jose better than anyone, and I thought I could turn to her for advice. "You were married to him, and you know all about the cheating and everything, and I wonder if you think it's ever going to change."

"It's not going to change," she said. "Jose is Jose. It's never going to change."

I kept going: "You know that time Jose went to see you in Miami, after your baby was born; he said you wanted to get back together."

"That's a lie," she said. "I would never get back together with Jose."

"I feel like I'm addicted to him," I confided.

"I was addicted to him, too," Esther said. "He's got that quality to him. But look at me: I got away from him, and I survived. My life has never been better."

By the time I got off the phone, I felt I was going to make it without him.

Then the season ended, and the trouble began. Even before Jose called me from Weston, I could almost *sense* that he was back in town. It was eerie, and it frightened me. He was home, and he wasn't calling me. Why not? Was there someone else? Had he given up on me?

Jesus, what was wrong with me?! Had I become addicted to the abuse? *I am not going back. Not, not, not, not, not!*

Jose finally called with another ultimatum. "If you don't want to reconcile, let me know now because I'm getting ready to move forward with someone else."

"There's someone else?"

"You heard me," he said. "This is my final attempt to save my family."

I went into panic mode, as Jose knew I would. The fact is that there was nobody else—not any *one* woman, anyway. He was back to his old ways, whoring around, and maybe it wasn't as satisfying as it used to be. He wanted his wife and daughter back. He could feel me vacillating.

"Here's the deal," he said. "You move back in, you can stay in school. You don't move back in, we're finished. It's over. End of story."

I caved. I hated myself for it, and the decision defied logic on every level, but there were two Jessicas: One was smart and logical; the other was an emotional wreck. The two of us had been doing battle for many years. I knew which one I liked better, but at the moment she was down for the count.

"I don't like the house in Weston," I told Jose. "It has too many bad memories. And it's too far from school. And we don't need something that extravagant anyway."

That was all he needed to hear. Within days, we started looking for a condo in Miami. We found a beautiful place on the water, in an exclusive building called The Santa Maria. I broke my lease, Josie and I moved in, and Jose brought Vera along. Vera was very sweet, though I'm sure she was conflicted. She had tried to protect me from Jose, and now I was back.

Jose got busy redoing the condo, which was already beautifully appointed, and I got busy with school. True to his word, he didn't get in the way of my education. I enjoyed my studies, and he enjoyed his self-appointed role as an interior decorator. The condo was modern, with clean lines, and he stuck to that motif. He didn't want any input from me, though. He was going to do everything himself.

The 1999 off-season flew by, and I began to wonder why I'd come back. I was happy in school, but when I got back to the condo I felt like I was living with a roommate, a disconnected, oblivious roommate. My unhappiness began to express itself in the old, familiar ways. First, I started shopping again, but even that had lost its allure.

I became increasingly depressed. I decided to have my nose redone. Again. I found another plastic surgeon and subjected myself to the knife. Then I decided that my boobs needed attention. Again. I had them done, too. There were better, more reliable implants on the market, and I wanted them.

I remained unhappy. Young as I was, I decided I needed BOTOX. Magically, my imaginary wrinkles disappeared, and I immediately felt better about myself. I was improving by leaps and bounds.

Shortly before Christmas, the attorneys called to discuss our divorce proceedings. We had spent so much money on them that we decided to let the law take its course. It was like a runaway train—neither of us had the energy to stop it. And really, at the end of the day, what difference did it make? We'd be divorced, but we'd continue living together as a couple.

On January 4, 2000, we were no longer man and wife. In other words, nothing had really changed.

The following month, Jose went back to spring training to get ready for his second season with Tampa. "You're coming with me," he said.

"Jose," I said. "I'm in school. I thought we had a deal."

"I don't care," he said. "I'm not going through this shit again. I want my family back. This going to school thing isn't working for me."

I dropped out, hating myself with every fiber of my being. I was numb with depression all season. I addressed the problem by looking even more closely at my physical self, searching for things to fix. I got hooked on BOTOX, even though my face was virtually free of wrinkles, and on collagen treatments, even though my lips were perfectly fine as they were.

I found a small mole on my shoulder and went for laser treatments to deal with the discoloration. I remember showing it to Vera, who couldn't see it. "What mole? Where?"

"It's right there," I insisted, as if she were blind. "It's horrendous."

It was practically microscopic, but I felt ugly and wanted to fix everything. I didn't realize that the problem was psychological, not physical.

Then I went back to the salon again. In the space of a week, I went from blonde to brunette and back to blonde again. Once, Jose rolled over in the middle of the night, saw me, and did a double take, waking with a start.

"What's wrong?" I asked.

"Nothing," he stammered. "I forgot where I was."

"What's that supposed to mean? You thought you were with someone else?"

"No, no," he protested. "I was just dreaming."

He would come home after his games, suffering from one injury or another, looking for an ice pack. At one point he was in so much pain that he couldn't put his socks on. He was eating Advil by the handful, and I kept pumping him full of steroids.

A lot of the players were coming by to visit in those days. I'm not going to name names—I'll leave that to Jose—but they were all there to get their fix.

I wasn't really interested, to be honest. I wasn't interested in the players, and I wasn't interested in the wives. I didn't want to be around anyone. I didn't want to pretend that I was happy. I didn't have the energy for the kind of playacting I needed simply to make it through the day.

I stayed with Josie. I read. I listened to music (Depeche Mode, U2, Delirium, Hooverphonics, and more). And I looked for more physical flaws.

Then it became apparent that Jose was cheating again. I'd find notes in his pocket, an unfamiliar lipstick in his car. And one time he called me, ostensibly from the golf course, but the number that popped up on the screen was from the 813 area code. I thought he was using some girl's phone and that her line was unblocked.

"Whose phone are you on?" I asked.

"*My* phone. What are you talking about?"

"You have a 305 phone. This is an 813."

"You're crazy," he said. "I'm on the golf course. Here!" He handed the phone to his assistant, who was playing golf with him and some friends, and she confirmed it. "He's on his phone, Jess. We're playing golf. Me and Jose and Ozzie and Glen. It's a beautiful day."

It kept happening, though. And when I called the number back, it would immediately kick over to a computerized voice, which instructed me to leave a message.

"I need to know what's going on, Jose," I said. "What is this 813 number that keeps popping up?"

"You're crazy!" he screamed at me. "You are going to ruin this relationship with your fucking craziness."

I began to wonder whether he was right. I called my mom and told her I needed help. "I think I'm losing my mind," I said. She suggested I try to find a therapist, and I took her advice.

I found someone in the phone book and made an appointment. He was a quiet, middle-aged guy. I described our troubled marriage, with as much detail as I could manage, and it took several sessions to get through the entire story. When I was done, he wanted to go further back, all the way back to my childhood. He began to point out the similarities between Jose and my father and between me and my mother. I didn't like what I was hearing. I said I was there to fix myself, not the rest of the world, at which point he said something I really didn't want to hear: "You don't really want to fix yourself, Jessica. If you fix yourself, you'll have to leave Jose. And you're not ready to leave Jose."

Maybe not, but I was ready to leave the therapist. If he was wrong, he was a quack. And if he was right, I was in more trouble than I knew.

But he'd put that crazy notion in my head, and I couldn't get it out of there. I told myself I was ready to leave Jose. I could work in the skin care field. I didn't have the degree I wanted, but the hours I'd already invested had earned me a somewhat lesser degree, and it was still good. I could get a decent job tomorrow, if I really wanted to. I wanted to talk to Jose about the possibility, but I was too afraid. I knew he would subject me to his usual litany: *I'm the provider here. Don't I take care of you? I need you at home! Stop pissing me off with your crazy ideas.*

We were sitting in the bedroom one night, watching TV. Jose was in his underwear, immobile, completely focused on the show.

For a moment, I was reminded of my father, in his own underwear, also glued to the TV. Then the phone rang. It was for Jose. This was late July, early August. He had been placed on waivers by the Devil Rays, meaning that they had basically given up on him as a player and were trying to get rid of him by unloading him on anyone who'd take him. He was chosen by the Yankees.

No one could figure out why the Yankees wanted him. He'd been having a lousy year. Then it became clear: They were only hiring him to keep him off the other teams. Jose Canseco was slowly going downhill, but he was still a dangerous force at bat. The team didn't really want him, but they didn't want to play against him.

At that moment, in another rare moment of clarity, I saw the parallels between the Yankees and myself. I didn't really want Jose either, but I didn't want to play against him.

End of Story

A week after Jose was picked up by the Yankees, we arrived in New York and began looking for an apartment. I didn't understand why I was still with him. The flesh is weak, they say, and—in my case—that definitely applied.

The entire New York experience turned into a nightmare. This was August, and there were only two months left in baseball season, and we couldn't find a decent, short-term lease. To make matters worse, the city was stiflingly hot.

We finally found a place on the Upper West Side. It was nothing to write home about, but it would have to do. Jose hated it. He hated New York. And he hated the Yankees. He spent what was left of the season on the bench.

I wasn't a big fan of New York either, but I made the best of it. I'd take Josie for long walks along the bustling streets, to Central Park, and even to a few Broadway shows. I was trying to turn each day into an adventure.

One afternoon, back at the apartment, I logged onto our computer—the laptop I shared with Jose—and an e-mail message popped up on the screen. "Hey! How are you? Haven't talked in a while. Do you still have my numbers?" It was signed by someone I'll call Gabrielle. I thought she was another cheap slut, eager to reconnect with Jose, but it was worse. Much worse. I called the number. A woman answered.

"Who's this?" I asked.

"Who's this?" she asked.

"This is Jose Canseco's wife."

There was a long pause. "This is Gabrielle," the woman said.

"I already figured that out," I replied. "You trying to reach my husband for any particular reason?"

"You have it all wrong," she said. "I'm not seeing Jose. I run an escort agency."

"What?!"

"And I'm sorry. I didn't know he was married."

I was stunned, but there was more to come. Apparently, Gabrielle had been dealing with Jose for many years, and he was a lousy client. He didn't believe in paying for sex, but he liked being set up with Gabby's girls. "He's incredibly arrogant," she told me, though I already knew that. "If he had his way, they'd be paying him."

"So why do you put up with it?"

"Because a lot of girls like his type," she said. "You'd be surprised."

No, actually. I wouldn't.

In the middle of the conversation, Jose returned from the ballpark. "Who are you talking to?" he asked.

"Your friend Gabrielle," I said. "You're asking her to set you up with girls?"

"Give me that phone!"

"You bastard," I said, suddenly in tears. "Why didn't you tell her you had a wife and kid at home?!"

"Give me the fucking phone!"

"You should leave him," Gabrielle said. "He's an asshole."

Jose moved toward me, but I warned him to stay back, and he knew better than to touch me. He stormed into the bedroom, slamming the door behind him.

"I'm sorry," Gabrielle said. "I didn't mean to hurt you."

I hung up and dried my tears, and I followed Jose into the bedroom. "Let me see your cell phone," I said. It turned out he had a second cell phone, one with an 813 prefix. I hadn't been wrong about that, either. Jose used it to call his little girlfriends, and of course that bill never reached our home. When I first confronted him about the number, that day on the golf course, he told me I was crazy, and he kept telling me I was crazy until I believed him.

"I want to hear your messages," I said. "Give me the code."

"No."

"If you don't give me the code, I'm walking out right now."

He gave me the code. I dialed in for his messages, punched in the code, and my worst fears were immediately confirmed. "Hey, Jose. It's Donna. You want to do something tonight?" "Hi, Jose, it's me. Let me know when you want me to fly to New York." "Jose, it's Jeannie. I miss you. Call me."

I was crying again. "So this is how it is?" I asked. "I drop out of school for you. I move to New York for you. I give up my life for you. And this is how you repay me? This is how you show how much you love me?"

He didn't say anything. He had trouble meeting my eyes. Usually he would concoct some bullshit story or apologize in some lame manner, but the evidence against him was overwhelming, so there was nothing to say. I left the room, wiped my tears, and booked a flight home for the following morning. What a twisted creep. It wasn't enough that women threw themselves at him; he had to push for freebies from a high-class escort service.

I slept in the other room. I was furious with Jose, but even more furious with myself. If I was still in love with this man, if I even *thought* I was still in love with him, he was right about me—I *was* crazy.

In the morning, before I left, he insisted on taking me to breakfast. "Please don't do this to me," he said, singing the same old song. "I love you so much. I'm asking you not to leave me."

"If this is love, I don't want anything to do with it."

"No. You don't understand. It's me. I'm a complete idiot. I have a problem. I'm going to fix it."

"When, Jose? We've been together for seven years, and it's only getting worse."

"Please, Jess. Those girls don't mean anything to me. It's an ego boost. You're the only woman I love. Please don't go. I don't want to lose my family. You and Josie are all I've got."

I returned to Miami, crippled by depression. I thought about having another nose job and looked into having my breasts redone, but I was in such bad shape that I couldn't even muster the energy for that.

Then one morning, as if by magic, I emerged from the fog and made a decision. I wasn't going to leave Jose. I was going to stay in the condo and focus on getting my life in order, and I would leave when I was good and ready to leave. What's more, I was going to live my life the way I wanted to live it. I would come and go as I pleased, when I pleased, where I pleased. I intended to show Jose that I could be as absent and disengaged as he was. And really, at this point, what could he say? I was in a position of strength. I had nothing to lose but Jose.

When Jose returned to Miami after that very short season, he knew immediately that something had changed. On his second night home, he walked into the bathroom and found me in front of my makeup mirror, getting ready for a night on the town.

"Where you going?" he asked

"Out," I said.

"With whom?"

"Friends."

"What friends?"

"The girls," I said. "The usual crowd."

When he began to protest, I ignored him, and I continued to ignore him even as he followed me down to corridor to the elevator. He was upset and angry, but mostly he was confused. "I don't understand," he said.

"There's nothing to understand," I said. "I'm going *out*."

He was asleep by the time I got home, and the next day he didn't say a word about it. I went about my morning as if nothing had happened, but on the inside I was grinning.

I went out again the following week and returned to the condo to find Jose on the bed, watching TV, with Josie fast asleep at his side. "So?" he asked, trying to act casual. "Where were you?"

"Oh, you know—had a few drinks with friends."

I began to undress. I was loving this.

When Halloween rolled around, he assumed we had no plans. But late in the evening I announced that I was going out, and I told him to try to put Josie to bed early.

"Hey!" he snapped. "I'm getting fucking tired of this!"

"Well, deal with it."

"Where the fuck are you going this time?"

"Wherever the fuck I want," I said. "Why? You going to kick me out?"

It was ugly, and I knew it wouldn't work long-term, but for the moment it was certainly empowering. Jose had fucked up big time. He had no choice but to take my shit. One wrong word out of him, and I was gone. And I was fine with that. More than fine. He's the one who wanted me there. I was running the show.

"How long is this going to go on?" he whined.

"Hey, Jose, I'm just living my life."

"I'm not going to take this shit from you," he said.

"So ask me to leave," I said. "It's easy. We're not married anymore, remember?"

In my heart and mind, I had already left Jose. I was going to stick around long enough to map out the next chapter of my life, and I was going to take my daughter, pack my bags, and leave. If he wanted to force me out early, I could live with that. The fact is that I didn't need him anymore.

This went on for several weeks—I would go to class, study, and spend an occasional evening out with my friends—and Jose accepted it, albeit grudgingly. Then one night he asked if he could join me. It was a wonderful moment. I was wearing the pants in the family. "Okay," I said. "But you have to promise not to be an asshole."

He actually behaved himself. We went out with my friends, who turned out to be a lot less trashy and disgusting than he thought, and we had a pleasant evening. To be completely honest, it was comforting to have Jose in the booth next to me. He was still as gorgeous and as sexy as ever, and I liked this new, somewhat emasculated version of Jose. He wasn't running the show anymore. We were on equal footing now. I think I can honestly say that for the first time in all our years together we were real partners. I even remember thinking: *This is what a marriage should be.*

Before long, we became part of a larger, hard partying crowd. We were out three and four nights a week, drinking too much, with the occasional hit of Ecstasy tossed in for good measure (for me, not for Jose). It was wild, mindless fun, but it took its toll. There were mornings when I couldn't drag myself to school; school suddenly seemed less important. In fact, the *future* seemed less important. All my big plans—how I was going to get my life in order, how I was going to leave Jose when I was good and ready to leave him—suddenly went up in smoke. I was happy. Or I *thought* I was happy. The fact is I was about to crash and burn.

One night, the combination of Ecstasy and alcohol made me feel a little too lovey-dovey for my own good. We were out with a group of people, including a close friend of mine, a beautiful girl, and—with only a vague awareness of what I was doing—I invited her back to the condo. I ended up sharing her with Jose.

A few weeks later, it happened again, with another close girlfriend. I took her aside before we left the bar and spelled it out for her. "I just want you to know that I'm okay with it if you want to be with Jose. I feel really close to you. I think it would be real nice."

Ecstasy is a dangerous drug. Under its influence, the world is a wonderful place. People are wonderful. You lose your inhibitions, and you also lose your mind.

When we got back to the condo, we all began fooling around together, and she was really into it. So was I. So was Jose. At one point, he turned to me and said, "Do you want me to fuck her?"

And I said, "Yes."

I watched them make love. Mostly I watched Jose's face. He looked so happy that it made me happy. I was doing this for him. I was procuring women for my man, to make my man happy. I never stopped to think that *I* should have been enough to make him happy—*more* than enough—because I didn't feel as if I was enough, and I didn't feel I ever would be.

On January 16, 2001, Jose signed as a free agent with the Anaheim Angels, and I saw this as a sign. I picked up the phone and called my old friend Jean Renard, who by this time had moved to Los Angeles.

"I'm coming out in the spring," I told him. "We're going to be living in Anaheim."

"Great," he said. "I can't wait to see you. Can you get out here any sooner? I'll set up some meetings."

I told Jose I was going to L.A.—I *told* him, I didn't ask him—and a week later, despite his whining, I was on my way.

Jean introduced me to an agent who wanted to sign me on the spot. I was thrilled. I knew L.A. was a hard town to crack, but I also knew I could do it.

When I got back to Miami, I was feeling pretty optimistic. I would move to Anaheim with Jose and Josie, and I'd make the short drive to Los Angeles whenever I needed to be there. It was perfect. Everything was falling into place. My life was finally beginning to work.

Things at home were working out, too. My relationship with Jose seemed like a whole new relationship. I had some power now. I was no longer the insecure nineteen-year-old girl who had fallen so hopelessly in love with him so many years ago. I was twenty-seven. I was a mother. And I was a partner. Most important, I was no longer afraid of losing him. If you love someone, you certainly don't want to lose them. But if you think your life depends on them, there's something wrong with the relationship. I was beginning to see that people shouldn't be together out of need; they should be together out of desire. And, believe it or not, I truly wanted to be with Jose. We had come through so much, and we had survived, and I was convinced that we were going to make it.

When we arrived in Scottsdale, Arizona, for spring training, my heart went out to Jose in other ways. The poor bastard was a mess. Sometimes I'd take Josie out to the ballpark and find Jose walking around with five ice packs taped to his body. Arm, leg, hamstring, back, shoulder. He looked ridiculous, and he knew he looked ridiculous. He was hurting big time.

There was a whole new set of baseball wives to meet, but they weren't any different from the baseball wives I'd met over the years. They would sit in their designated seats, waving at their men, then turn their attention to the groupies in the stands. They would check them out, one at a time, and the groupies would check the wives out right back. Both sets of women were more bitchily curious about one another than about anything that was happening on the playing field, and it was entertaining to watch. The baseball wives were invariably anxious. They knew what types of women their men were attracted to, so they knew what to look for when they scanned the stands. I had been no different. I had scanned the stands with the rest of them, and whenever I saw Jose's type—young, blonde, fit—my heart would skip a beat. But at that point I wasn't even looking at them. Jose's cheating days were over. I felt pretty cocky. I felt like the only woman there who had absolutely nothing to worry about.

I was feeling so cocky, in fact, that I began to accompany Jose to the local strip clubs. Jose got a kick out of it. It also turned him on, and that turned me on, and it added an odd little fantasy element to our sex lives.

But one night everything went to hell. We were back from a strip club, getting ready for bed, when Jose showed his true colors. "When are we going to bring home another girl?" he asked.

I turned to look at him, feeling weak-kneed and winded. *When are we going to bring home another girl*? What the hell was wrong with him? I thought that was behind us. Whenever I thought back to what we had done in Miami, I didn't think of it with pride. Twisted as it sounds, those little sexual escapades had helped us reconnect, but the shame remained lodged deep inside me. I lived with what we'd done because there was no undoing it, but I certainly wasn't about to repeat it. Jose, however, didn't seem to have a problem with it.

"Are you serious?" I asked.

"Why not?"

I shook my head, stunned by his cluelessness. "Jose," I said, "what happened in Miami was wrong. We invited people into our bedroom, and we let them share in the most intimate part of our lives. And the only positive thing I can say about it is that at least they weren't complete strangers. But now you're telling me that you want to do it again, and that you're happy to pick up any random girl—maybe even a stripper—and bring her into our bedroom?"

"Why are you making such a big deal out of it?"

"Because it *is* a big deal!"

"I thought you liked it!"

"No!" I said. "It was fucked up. Can't you see that?"

"It was your idea!" he snapped.

He had a point. Initially, it *had* been my idea—an idea fueled by alcohol and drugs. And sure, it shook things up and got us back on track, but now it became clear that we had paid too high a price. In trying to save the relationship, we had done so much damage that we would never recover. In our mutual desperation, we had lost our way, but there was one big difference: He was still lost. I wasn't.

A few days later, without making a big deal out of it, I calmly packed my bags and took Josie with me to Miami. The following week before the season even started, Jose was released by the Angels. He had been injured, and he followed us home. The only offer he got that year was from the Newark Bears, an independent minor league team in Newark, New Jersey. He was crushed, and I felt bad, but I wasn't there for him emotionally. I had already left him. His behavior had determined how our story would turn out, and I was quietly writing the final chapter.

Finally, I broke it to him. "I'm moving to Los Angeles," I said.

"What are you talking about?"

"I'm taking Josie, and I'm moving to L.A."

"The fuck you are," he said. "Read the fine print."

Jose was referring to our divorce agreement, which hadn't been made public. In fact, a lot of people weren't even aware that we *had* divorced. I had agreed to stay in Florida until Josie was eighteen, knowing that I would never abandon her. Now Jose was resorting to threats. If I wanted to go to Los Angeles, I'd be doing so without my daughter.

Jose went off to New Jersey, and he did everything in his power to keep me from leaving Miami. I left anyway, and I took Josie with me, and once a month—come hell or high water—I would fly her out and let her spend a few days with Jose. Every time I showed up, Jose would ask me to stay, suggesting that we could make things right between us, begging me for one last chance. But I was finished with him. Things had never been right between us, and I knew they never would be.

Jose was furious. He hated the fact that I was finally taking control of my life, and he was particularly upset to learn that I had hit the ground running. Less than two months after I arrived in L.A., I was modeling—doing print jobs and catalog work. And a month after that, I did a national commercial for Coors Light.

It was the most liberating time of my life. I was not only free, but also working and loving it. And I was being smart about working: I took some of that money and enrolled in Santa Monica College. I decided to study nursing, as my mother had done. I had no intention of giving up modeling, and I was even going to try acting, but I wanted something to fall back on if my career didn't pan out. Nursing seemed like a solid foundation.

I felt terrific. I felt, in fact, as if I was living someone's else dream. I was truly free. I didn't need Jose. I had myself. And I could be anything I set my mind to be.

Don't get me wrong: There were many moments of doubt and pain. And I did a few things with my newfound freedom—sexual and otherwise—of which I am not particularly proud.

There were moments of sadness, too. I had put more than eight years of my life into that relationship, and, on some level, the end of any relationship is an acknowledgment of failure. But failure is just life's way of preparing you for success. And I was ready for success. Every day away from Jose, I felt a little stronger. Every day I was finding new sources of nourishment: work, friendship, school, motherhood.

Jose was still in the picture, though, and he always would be: We shared a daughter. For a time, he engaged me in a bitter custody battle, perhaps thinking that he'd wear me down and persuade me to reconcile. I had gone back in the past, more often than I cared to remember, but it wasn't going to happen this time.

I felt bad for Jose but not *that* bad. I felt bad about his dwindling prospects as a professional ballplayer, and I felt even worse when he and Ozzie got into a fight at a Florida bar that made headlines across the country. His life seemed to be spiraling out of control, and my prospects had never looked better.

Eventually, Jose called off the lawyers. He didn't need Josie and me to go back to Florida; he had decided to try his luck in California. I was thrilled—for Josie, if not for me. After all, every kid deserves two parents.

Being a mother has been the most rewarding experience of my life. It has also taught me things about my own childhood that I am only now beginning to understand. A generation ago, my mother was a girl just like me—lost, insecure, married to the wrong man, and struggling to find her way. She made a lot of progress throughout the years; I'd like to think that I've made a little progress myself.

Sure, I've made more than my share of mistakes. I went to insane lengths to make my marriage work, and I'm not using the word loosely. I was crazy, crazy in love, or what I thought was love. I was addicted to Jose Canseco, and like any addict I would do anything to get my fix. That wasn't love, though. It held the promise of love, but I was young and inexperienced, and I couldn't see beyond my feelings. I let myself become another person, a person I didn't much like. I went against my own best instincts, and—for a while—I completely lost my way.

But I'm back now. For me and for my daughter. One of the amazing things about having a child is the way it literally changes your center of gravity, which is a *good* thing. In this self-absorbed culture, there's nothing quite like a child to put your life into perspective.

I am working very hard on being a good mother, and I am

also working on myself. When I was with Jose, I would look into his eyes to see what was reflected there, and I relied on him to tell me who I was. When he was unhappy with me, I was miserable. When he went off with other women, I blamed myself. And when he belittled me, I clung to him more desperately than ever, determined to change his mind. But now I see that I was wrong to give him that kind of power. The only person who has a right to stand in judgment of me is me. I'm working on that, and I'm proceeding cautiously, especially when it comes to men. I will continue to trust my heart, certainly, but I'll also be sure to use my head.

If I have learned anything from this experience, it is this: Do not look to others to tell you what you're worth. Only you can determine your value as a person. At the end of the day, life is about becoming responsible for yourself and your own happiness. That is what I am trying to do, and I am doing it one small step at a time.

Afterword

Life after Jose hasn't always been easy. I was out on my own for the first time ever and that took a lot of adjusting to. And it wasn't just about me anymore. I had a daughter to take care of, and I was determined—like every mother is—to be the best mother in the world.

I found good schools for Josie, who's in third grade as of this book's publication and thriving. Just as important, Jose is living in Los Angeles, so Josie has both of us in her life, and she knows that we both love her.

As for me, I'm focusing on modeling and acting—I am on the September 2005 cover of *Playboy*—and I'm still inching my way toward a nursing degree. I'm also developing a line of skin care products with a local doctor. When the time comes, we hope to market our products on the Internet.

I've also been in therapy, working on understanding the forces that shaped me and on what I can do to become a better person. I was in a lot of pain for much of my time with Jose, and almost by default I've become something of an expert on addictive relationships. I have two words for any woman who is stuck in a similar situation:

Get out.

The fact is, life *does* go on, things *do* get better, and there really *is* a light at the end of the tunnel. It all comes down to taking that first step—and taking it again and again and again until you finally manage to break free.

I broke free and went back more times than I care to count—the distinguishing marks of a true addict—but I'm finally on my own, and I have never in my entire life felt happier or better about myself.

As for Jose, he is Josie's father, and he will always be a part of our lives. Some days will be better than others, I'm sure, but I'm not worried about them.

Life is best lived one day at a time.

Acknowledgments

I have a great many people to thank, so I'll begin at the beginning.

Mom: I couldn't have made it without you. It took us a while to figure things out, but you turned into the greatest mother in the world. Thank you for your love and support, and thank you for your faith in me. I'm sorry about Dad. He did the best he could. I love you, Mom.

Samantha, my big sister: You are real fine, Sammy. Thanks for being so supportive, and thanks also for all the laughs with you and Smith. I love you.

Rachel, my little sister: You have always been my special Poe. I love stirring up trouble with you and reminiscing about our childhood. I'm sorry about Bunny's arm. I love you.

Jean Renard: Thank you for believing in me. You helped me more than you know.

Angela, my best friend: Well, we did it, girl! We moved to L.A. Thank you for giving me the courage to do it. Some day the dream about the house with the animals will really come true.

Kacey: Thanks for being understanding, Mo, and for always being there for me.

Barry: Thanks for helping me through a difficult time. You have no idea how much it meant.

Sebastian: Thanks for being a great guy and for putting up with the cats. We'll be friends till the end.

Ira: You have been a great friend. I wish you the best of luck in life.

Teresa and Barbie: Thanks for trying. I will never forget your support.

Jamie: I know I don't always listen to you, but you mean the world to me. Thank you.

Judith Regan and Doug Grad: Thank you for giving me a chance to tell my story.

Pablo Fenjves: Thank you for making this happen. You are the best!

Steve: My thanks to you and Century Talent for all of your hard work on my behalf. I know there are great things in store for us!

Charif: You know why.

Mark: Wow! You are amazing. *Je t'aime.*

STEROIDS, SEX AND FOUL BALL
PLAYBOY
ENTERTAI
.playboy.com • SEPTEMBER
JOSE'S
JESSIC
CANSEC
TELLS ALL SHOW
AL
THE WILD LI
OF A BIG LEAGUE W
IT'S BA
PLAYBO
FEARLE
COLLEGE FOOTBALL FORECA
THE TOP 25
TEAM
YBOY
INTERVIEW: THOMAS L. FRIEDMAN
NASCAR'S KURT BUSCH PETE CARROLL
VINTAGE ROADSTERS NEW PLAYBOY FASHION
INVESTMENT TIPS IRAQI BOMB SQUAD

The happy princess, the king, and the not-so-happy queen

Josie hugs Raymond, the Tampa Bay Devil Rays mascot.

Josie in second grade

Me and my sisters—Sam (*center*) and Rachel (*right*)—in Washington State, 2000

Vera, Jose's loyal housekeeper

Josie and I get ready to go out.

Proud papa Jose gives Josie a bottle.

Jose sitting silently on the couch, being depressed. This was what he was like when he went off steroids.

Lean on me . . .

A very comfortable place

In happier times, with Jose by the boat

At my wedding shower with Jose's sister, Teresa

Showing off my new outie bellybutton

"You may kiss the groom." Jose and I were married in bed.

I love animals—including cougars.

This breakfast is for the birds. Jose loves animals, too.

Jose and I make time for the iguana so he doesn't get too jealous after the baby is born.

Libby and Buffy

Jose in black underwear, like when I showed up at his hotel room on our first "date." Note the scar

My entry picture for the 1993 Fitness America Pageant—very patriotic

Getting ready for a night on the town in New York City

© George Remington

At the NCSA Ballet School in 1985—en pointe

My first modeling job—for the 1986 Taffy's-By-Mail dancewear catalog

Senior year of high school homecoming court, escorted by Dad. Love that hair!

The Ohio farmhouse—my childhood home and home to some shocking secrets

Hanging out with Mom when I was about five years old

Me in second grade. Even then I liked the camera!

My parents, B.C. (before children)

Dad sitting around in his underwear—as usual

The Sekely family, circa late 1970s: me, Dad, Mom, Samantha, and Rachel